GRATITUDE
IN THE REAR VIEW
MIRROR

John L. Hurlbut

ISBN

Hardcover: 978-1-966902-15-7

Paperback: 978-1-966902-16-4

Gratitude in the Rear-View Mirror is a heartfelt and introspective memoir that gently invites readers into the life of John Linwood Hurlbut—a journey shaped by faith, reflection, and the transformative power of gratitude. With a conversational tone and deeply personal storytelling, the book engages readers not through spectacle, but through honesty, warmth, and wisdom. Each chapter serves as a vignette that uncovers how life's challenges, viewed through the rearview mirror of time, often reveal unexpected blessings.

More than a memoir, Gratitude in a Rear-View Mirror serves as a spiritual guidepost for readers navigating their own moments of uncertainty, loss, and growth. In a world often focused on immediacy and outcomes, Hurlbut's reflections champion the long view—where the real meaning of events often becomes clear only in hindsight. Through scripture-infused insights and personal anecdotes, the book emphasizes how faith and gratitude can coexist with hardship, shaping a more grounded and grateful life perspective

ABOUT THE AUTHOR

John Hurlbut has embraced authorship in his later years, publishing his first book, *Citizen Can*, at 76. One year later, he followed with *Gratitude in the Rear-View Mirror*. These two works share key themes, as *Citizen Can* explores the principles of good citizenship and the pursuit of a higher level of mutual existence. This book aligns seamlessly with *Gratitude in the Rear-View Mirror*, as both emphasize reflection, personal growth, and the lasting influence of past experiences in shaping a better future.

A product of the public school system in rural Virginia, John honorably served his country in Vietnam before earning his degree from Fordham University in New York City. There, he met his lifelong partner of more than 50 years. His distinguished career spans roles as a public accountant, internal audit manager, corporate controller, chief financial officer, and Executive Director of two nonprofit organizations.

In both books, John attributes his understanding of good citizenship, rooted in Love and the Golden Rule, to his grandmother's guidance. These core values have given him direction and a sense of purpose throughout his life. John has a supportive wife, Nena, two adult children, Greg and Kathy, and two cherished grandchildren, Ryan and Ethan.

ACKNOWLEDGMENTS

No journey is traveled alone, and this book is a testament to the many people and places that have shaped my life, values, and sense of gratitude.

First and foremost, my life would not have started as well as it did without the love, nurturing, and guidance I received in my early years from **Mama Kitty and Uncle Jack** and later, during my maturing years, from my **mother, Dorothy, and stepfather, Herbert**. Their unwavering support laid the foundation for the person I am today.

I extend my most profound appreciation to **Fordham University**. This institution welcomed me and instilled in me the discipline, diligence, and perseverance that guided me through my career and personal life. It was at Fordham that I learned the value of applying myself. I remain ever grateful to the professors and mentors who encouraged me to shift my focus from marketing to accounting. This decision profoundly shaped my future.

Fordham was also where I met the love of my life, my wife of 52 years. She has been the heart of our family, which has grown to include our two successful children, **Greg and Kathy**, and Kathy's wonderful family --- her husband, **Adam,** and our two cherished grandchildren, **Ryan** and **Ethan.**

To my wife's family, **the Unchuans**, I owe an immeasurable debt of gratitude. Their love, wisdom, and values --- acceptance, nurturing, intelligence, professionalism, fairness, and fun --- have enriched my life in ways I never imagined. Their unwavering support has been a beacon of strength, and I am truly blessed to call them family.

I have been fortunate to cross paths with many remarkable people. While I cannot name them all, I would like to acknowledge a few who have had a meaningful impact on my life: **Frank and**

Tracey DiSanto, Lee and Liz Durham, Paul Terlemezian, Jim and Melissa Wade, and my bridge network—including Claudia, Sue, Joyce, another Joyce, Roger, and Vicki --- along with Lee Durham. I know God is welcoming Lee, who passed recently at age 94. The friendship and support from all of you have meant the world to me.

Life presents its challenges, and my journey with **prostate cancer** has been no exception. While this path has brought fear, sadness, stress, and uncertainty, it has also been illuminated by the love, care, and encouragement of those who have stood beside me. I extend my deepest gratitude to the medical professionals who have guided me through treatment and to the friends and family who have offered compassion and reassurance.

Since writing *Citizen Can*, I have been fortunate to reconnect with a few of my **high school classmates**, most notably **Tom, Gwen, and Marguerite**, whose kindness and friendship have meant so much.

I cannot conclude this section without expressing my gratitude to ChatGPT, which aided in my research and helped refine my text, ensuring it was presented in a manner befitting an experienced author.

Above all, I am deeply grateful for the countless moments of kindness, wisdom, and grace that have shaped my perspective. This book reflects not just my experiences but a tribute to the extraordinary people and places that have left an indelible mark on my heart.

With profound appreciation,
John L. Hurlbut

PREFACE

Life is a journey best understood in hindsight. Looking back through the rearview mirror of my experiences, I see a road paved with challenges, triumphs, love, and lessons learned. Gratitude has been my guiding light --- shaping my perspective, strengthening my resolve, and deepening my appreciation for the people and moments that have defined my path.

This book is not just a reflection on my past but a tribute to the individuals, circumstances, and values that have enriched my life. From my time in Vietnam to my formative years at Fordham University, from the family that welcomed me with open arms to the career that gave me purpose, each chapter is a testament to the power of resilience, faith, and gratitude.

Even in the face of hardship --- whether personal struggles, professional challenges, or my ongoing battle with cancer --- I have found reasons to be thankful. Adversity has tested me, but it has also revealed the depth of my strength and the unwavering support of those around me.

Gratitude in the Rear View Mirror is my way of acknowledging the past, embracing the present, and looking toward the future with hope. I hope that through my reflections, you, too, will find inspiration to appreciate the journey you've traveled and the blessings that surround you, even in the most unexpected places.

With gratitude,
John L. Hurlbut

CONTENTS

INTRODUCTION

Life has a way of moving forward, whether we are ready or not. We chase dreams, navigate hardships, and often don't take the time to pause and reflect on how far we have come. But when we glance in the rear-view mirror of our past, we may find something unexpected: gratitude.

This book explores the moments, people, and experiences that, in hindsight, have shaped us in ways we never anticipated. Some lessons arrived wrapped in joy, while others came disguised as challenges. Yet, through it all, there were gifts, i.e., hidden blessings, that only became apparent with time and perspective.

Gratitude in the Rear View Mirror is not just about looking back; it's about understanding, healing, and embracing the journey that has brought us to where we are today. It's a reminder that even in our struggles, there is something to be thankful for.

Gratitude in the Rear View Mirror is my second book. My first, *Citizen Can*, was published last year at age 76. The two books align in a few critical ways. Given that *Citizen Can* explores the values of good citizenship and achieving a higher level of mutual existence, it connects with Gratitude in the Rear View Mirror meaningfully: both books emphasize reflection, growth, and the impact of past experiences on shaping a better future. Specifically, they align perfectly in the following areas:

1. *Perspective on Progress*: Gratitude in the Rear View Mirror appreciates personal and collective experiences. At the same time, *Citizen Can* highlights how those experiences shape responsible, engaged citizens. Both encourage learning from the past to build a better future.
2. *The Role of Gratitude in Citizenship*: Good citizenship often involves recognizing the contributions of others, appreciating shared struggles, and acknowledging the

progress made as a society. *Citizen Can* emphasizes active participation in improving communities. At the same time, Gratitude in the Rear View Mirror encourages appreciating the journey that has led us to this point.

3. *Personal and Collective Growth*: Gratitude in the Rear View Mirror explores personal transformation through reflection, while *Citizen Can* focus on how individuals can transform their communities through values like respect, responsibility, and empathy. Both books suggest that looking back helps us move forward with greater purpose.

In essence, Gratitude in the Rear View Mirror provides the reflective lens, while *Citizen Can* offers the roadmap for action. Together, they create a powerful narrative about personal and societal evolution.

As you turn these pages, I invite you to reflect on your past, not regretfully, but with appreciation. Sometimes, the things we once saw as obstacles are the experiences that led us to our most significant growth. As I mentioned in *Citizen Can*, I am not an expert. I am a sinner, have been self-destructive, am a recovering alcoholic, have questioned God, and made several other mistakes. However, during my extensive life, many people impacted me in a way that allowed me to turn the pages of my bad behavior and create new pages of good behavior.

Gratitude has played a significant role in my transformation. It has given me the comfort that I am not alone. It has allowed me to see the good in others and go beyond what I have considered harmful. It has reduced my stress and enabled me to accept situations that I cannot control and develop a positive way to approach challenges that I may be able to tackle. In essence, I am happier and more able to be there for others when they call for my help.

Welcome to the journey.

1

G_{OD}

"A grateful mind is a great mind which eventually attracts to itself great things."
— *Plato*

"Life can only be understood backwards, but it must be lived forwards."
— *Soren Kierkegaard*

I start my journey on gratitude by quoting two of the most influential philosophers in history: Plato and Kierkegaard. The essence of their works provides critical insight into faith, Christianity, and even atheism (non-believing in a God or gods). Let's take a look at who they were.

Plato lived a few centuries before the birth of Jesus Christ. He was a Greek philosopher and one of the most influential thinkers in Western philosophy. He was a student of Socrates and the teacher of Aristotle, forming a foundational link in the development of philosophical thought. Plato wrote extensively on ethics, politics, metaphysics, epistemology, and aesthetics.

Plato believed in a higher, rational order that governed the universe. Still, his concept of divinity differed from Greek mythology's gods. His thoughts include: (1) a "Craftsman-God" orders the universe according to perfect Forms. This is not a personal God but a rational principle shaping reality. (2) Plato saw "The Good" as the highest principle, similar to a divine force. (3) He believed in the soul's immortality and that it goes through cycles of reincarnation. This suggests a belief in an eternal spiritual reality beyond the material world.

Although Plato was religious in a philosophical sense, he also engaged with skeptical and atheistic views at the time. Examples are: (1) He criticized Greek mythology and the immoral behavior of the Gods depicted by Homer. He sought a more rational and moral concept of the divine. (2) Plato argues that disbelief in the gods could lead to moral corruption and disorder. However, he acknowledges that not all atheists are immoral; some reject gods for philosophical reasons. (3) Unlike blind faith, Plato encouraged reasoning about divine things. His teleological view (believing the universe has purpose and order) would later influence arguments on God's existence.

A global look at Plato's works would probably reveal that he does not fit neatly into either side of the faith vs atheism debate. His belief in a rational divine order makes him different from traditional theists. Still, his emphasis on a higher reality beyond the physical world separates him from strict materialistic atheism.

Soren Kierkegaard's works are more recent. He was a 19th-century Danish philosopher who founded "Christian Existentialism," a philosophy emphasizing the individual's subjective relationship with God, focusing on faith, choice, and personal responsibility. His thought revolves around the idea that true Christianity is not just about intellectual belief but a "leap of faith," an existential commitment to God that goes beyond reason.

Kierkegaard described three progressive stages of human life: (1) Aesthetic Stage --- A life of pleasure, seeking enjoyment, and avoiding deeper meaning. (2) Ethical Stage --- A commitment to moral duty and responsibility. (3) Religious Stage --- A personal and passionate relationship with God, where one fully surrenders to faith.

In essence, Christian existentialism, in Kierkegaard's view, is about an individual's personal and sometimes agonizing journey toward authentic faith in God, requiring deep commitment, struggle, and, ultimately, a leap beyond human understanding.

Kierkegaard also had thoughts about atheism. He did not argue against atheism in a direct, systematic way. Still, Kierkegaard saw it as a state of existential crisis --- a failure to embrace one's self concerning God. However, he also respected the intellectual seriousness of those who rejected faith and saw their struggle as part of the journey toward authentic belief.

The philosophical thoughts of Plato and Kierkegaard provide a proper segue into this chapter's dive into faith and how gratitude feeds it.

Faith And Gratitude

Faith and gratitude are two profound forces shaping human experience, guiding us through life's uncertainties and blessings. Together, they create a powerful collaboration, reinforcing resilience, deepening joy, and fostering a sense of purpose.

Faith is the unseen thread that connects us to hope and perseverance. It is belief in something greater than ourselves, a conviction that there is a path forward even in the face of challenges. Faith is not merely a religious concept; it is a principle that transcends spiritual boundaries and manifests in trust --- trust in ourselves, others, and the unfolding journey of life.

A person with faith does not require immediate evidence of success; instead, they persist with the knowledge that their efforts and beliefs will bear fruit in time. Faith allows individuals to overcome hardships, take risks, and pursue their dreams despite obstacles. In times of difficulty, faith provides solace, reminding us that trials are temporary and that growth often arises from diversity.

Gratitude, on the other hand, is the practice of recognizing and appreciating the good in our lives. It shifts our focus from what we lack to what we have, fostering a mindset of abundance rather than scarcity. Gratitude transforms ordinary moments into treasures, allowing us to experience more profound commitment and fulfillment.

When we cultivate gratitude, we train our minds to notice and cherish the beauty around us --- a kind word, a shared laugh, a smile, a lesson learned. This practice enhances our well-being and strengthens our relationships, as appreciation fosters kindness and generosity.

Faith and gratitude are deeply intertwined. Faith enables us to trust that even our hardships serve a greater purpose. At the same time, gratitude allows us to find meaning and blessings within those challenges. Together, they help us navigate life with a heart full of hope and an outlook rooted in positivity.

When we have faith, we can see beyond immediate struggles and trust in the unfolding of our journey. Gratitude, in turn, keeps us grounded, helping us acknowledge the beauty and lessons found in every experience. This harmony between faith and appreciation creates a resilient and joyful spirit that gracefully embraces life's uncertainties.

Building a life rich in faith and gratitude requires intentional practice. Here are a few ways to nurture these qualities.

1. Reflect Daily – Acknowledge your gratitude and reaffirm your faith in the journey ahead.
2. Keep a Gratitude Journal – Writing down blessings, big or small, reinforces a positive mindset.
3. Surround Yourself with Positivity – Engage with people, books, and experiences that uplift and inspire faith and appreciation.

4. Practice Acts of Kindness – Sharing your gratitude and faith through kind deeds enriches both your life and the lives of others.
5. Embrace Challenges as Growth Opportunities – View hardships as steppingstones, trusting that they contribute to your personal and spiritual growth.

In conclusion, faith and gratitude are essential companions on the path of life. They provide strength in hardship, joy in abundance, and a deeper understanding of our place in the world. By embracing both, we cultivate a mindset that sees beauty in every season of life, knowing that each moment carries purpose and grace, whether triumphant or challenging.

Seeing God's Presence In The Past

Life is often understood best in hindsight. Sometimes, we wonder where God is in our struggles, but when we look back, we realize He was there all along. The past, though unchangeable, is a testimony to God's presence, guiding, shaping, and sustaining us through every situation.

In difficult times, it can feel like God is distant. Yesterday's trials may have seemed unbearable, but as we reflect, we see His fingerprints in the details. Think about moments of hardship that, in hindsight, led to unexpected blessings. Those closed doors, painful losses, or detours often reveal God's more fantastic plan when viewed from a distance.

Even in suffering, God was present. The moments we thought we were alone, He was carrying us. A person looks back on their life and sees only one set of footprints during the hard times. When asking God why, He responds, *"It was then that I carried you."* This phrase comes from a popular Christian poem: The Footprints in the Sand.

The past is not just a record of events – it is a classroom where God teaches us about His faithfulness. Reflection leads to gratitude. Our faith in the future grows when we recall how He provided, protected, and led us.

Instead of dwelling on regret, looking back should lead us to worship. *The Israelites built altars of remembrance* to recall what God had done. We, too, should mark moments of divine intervention and thank Him. Your gratitude journal is an appropriate place for this.

To summarize, we need to look back to move forward. God was there, even when we didn't see Him. He worked in silence, through the trials, and in our joys. As we look to the past, we gain confidence for the future, knowing that the same God who walked with us before will continue to guide us ahead.

"Jesus Christ is the same yesterday and today and forever."
(Hebrews 13:8)

Gratitude is often associated with religious belief but not exclusive to theists. Atheists and even agnostics experience deep thankfulness for life, love, experiences, and wonders of the universe. The absence of belief in a divine being does not diminish the depth or significance of gratitude; instead, it directs it toward the tangible and the present.

For theists, gratitude is often directed toward God, but for atheists, gratitude does not require a supernatural source. Instead, it is an appreciation for life, the people who shape our journey, and the random yet beautiful forces that brought us into existence.

Atheists often find gratitude in knowledge --- the ability to understand the universe and appreciate its complexity without needing divine explanations. They see that gravity holds the planets in orbit, that evolution has shaped life, and that human consciousness allows us to reflect is a source of profound appreciation.

Gratitude has psychological and social benefits that transcend religion. Studies show that practicing gratitude increases happiness, relationships, and well-being. Furthermore, research in positive psychology shows that gratitude improves mental health, regardless of religious belief. Acts of gratitude in a secular life include things such as writing thank-you notes, keeping a gratitude journal, or simply acknowledging the contributions of others, which fosters connection and fulfillment.

One of the common questions atheists face is, "How do you find meaning without God?" The answer often lies in embracing the fleeting nature of life. Without belief in an afterlife, many atheists cherish each moment more deeply, knowing that time is limited. In addition, love, friendships, and shared experiences become even more precious when seen as part of a finite existence.

In some religious traditions, gratitude is tied to the hope of divine rewards. Atheists often practice gratitude purely for its intrinsic value --- appreciating life not because of an expectation of eternal reward but because of the joy that gratitude brings. The existentialist thinker Albert Camus wrote about embracing life's absurdity with pleasure and finding beauty in simple moments. Gratitude often leads to action, whether through helping others, supporting causes, or simply acknowledging the goodness around us.

While religious dogma emphasizes faith, divine authority, and supernaturalism, atheism focuses on reason, evidence, and the natural world. Both offer frameworks for understanding existence but approach questions of life, morality, and meaning in fundamentally different ways

In closing, gratitude is not a religious monopoly. Whether one believes in God or not, appreciating life's moments, cherishing relationships, and finding joy in the universe remains universal. Atheism does not negate gratitude --- it enriches it, grounding it in the here and now, in the reality of existence, and in the deep appreciation for the fleeting, beautiful moments that make life meaningful.

I would like, at this point, to provide you with the following three stories that demonstrate my high level of gratitude for God's influence on my life.

A Love That Stood The Test Of Time

In the fall of 1969, Fordham University was alive with the energy of a generation on the cusp of change. The Bronx campus buzzed with students eager to make their mark on the world. Little did I know my world would be transformed forever.

I vividly remember the day- the crisp autumn air, the golden leaves crunching underfoot, and the hum of conversation in the quad. I was just another student (a few years older than the others due to my military service) navigating the whirlwind of classes and aspirations when fate intervened. That was the day I met HER.

She wasn't just another face in the crowd. There was something about her --- a quiet confidence, an effortless grace. Maybe it was the way she laughed or the kindness in her eyes when she spoke. Whatever it was, I was drawn to her, as if the universe had nudged me in her direction.

What started as casual conversations between classes quickly grew into something more profound. We spent hours walking around the campus, discussing our dreams, families, and hopes for the future. We studied together in the library, stole moments of laughter between lectures, and found comfort in each other during uncertain times.

Fordham was more than just a university to us --- it was where our story began. It became a place where two young hearts found each other amidst the chaos of exams, protests, and late-night coffee runs. It was where we built the foundation for something that would last a lifetime. We were a couple from different parts of the world. I grew up in a small town in Virginia, while she was born in a large city in the Philippines.

As years passed, life brought its challenges and joys. We built a home, raised a family, and weathered storms together. But through it all, I never forgot that first moment --- the day I met the woman who would become my wife, partner, and greatest blessing, my Nena forever.

Now, 55+ years later, I look at her and see the same woman who stole my heart on the Fordham campus. The same warmth, kindness, and laughter filled my life with immeasurable joy.

I am grateful every day for that moment in 1969- the twist of fate that brought us together, the love that grew from a single meeting on a college campus, and the incredible life we have built.

Fordham educated us, but importantly, it gave me HER. And for that, I will always be thankful.

A Family's Love: My Gratitude To Mama Kitty, My Mother, And Uncle Jack

Looking back on my early years, I realize just how much love surrounded me --- even in the absence of a father, who divorced my mom when I was less than one year old. While some may see a missing piece, I now see an entire life shaped by three incredible people who stepped in, not out of obligation but pure, unwavering love.

Mama Kitty, my grandmother, was the heart of the home. She only had a 6th-grade education, but she carried the wisdom of generations, her hands always busy --- whether kneading dough, mending clothes, or wiping away a child's tears. She taught me the importance of kindness, patience, and doing what's right even when no one is watching. Her love was steady, unconditional, and filled with the quiet strength that only grandmothers possessed. In my book Citizen Can, I emphasized two of Mama Kitty's life lessons: Love and the Golden Rule. I regularly reinforce these principles to my grandchildren.

I only saw my mother a few weeks out of every year in my formative years. After her divorce, she moved to New York City from the small town in Virginia where I was born and continued to live with my Mama Kitty. There, she was able to earn more money as a Registered Nurse and provide better financial support for my growth. She worked tirelessly to give me the best life, balancing responsibilities with a grace I didn't fully appreciate until I was older. She showed me what resilience looked like --- how to keep moving forward even when life threw obstacles in the way. Through every sacrifice, every late night, every moment of doubt, she never wavered in her love for me. She made sure I knew I was never alone.

Then there was Uncle Jack. He wasn't just an uncle --- he was a mentor, a role model, a father figure rolled into one. He taught me things every young boy needs to know- how to throw a ball, stand up for myself, and be honorable in a world that often tests a man's character. He was firm but fair, always encouraging, always present. He didn't have to take on that role, but he did without hesitation, and I will always be grateful.

Together, they gave me a childhood filled with warmth, laughter, and lessons that shaped the man I became. They taught me that love isn't about who is supposed to be there --- it's about who chooses to be there.

I owe so much to Mama Kitty, my mother, and Uncle Jack. They didn't just raise me --- they shaped me, supported me, and filled my life with a love so strong that I never felt the absence of what I didn't have.

To them, may they rest in peace. I am forever grateful.

Lessons From Vietnam: A Year That Shaped Me

Some moments in life define us --- experiences that change how we see the world and the way we see ourselves. My year in Vietnam was one of those moments. I was luckier than most since I spent my year as a Communications Center Specialist at a central relay station in Da Nang and not in armed combat.

I arrived young (I turned 21 that year), with the weight of duty on my shoulders but little understanding of what lay ahead. War has a way of stripping away illusions, revealing the raw truth of human nature- it's capacity for destruction and resilience, fear and courage, sorrow and brotherhood.

Vietnam was more than just a battlefield; it was a lesson in life itself. I learned the value of camaraderie- the kind not forged in words but in shared hardship. The men beside me were more than fellow soldiers; they were brothers. We carried each other through long nights and uncertain days, through moments of terror and fleeting moments of peace. That bond, that unspoken understanding, is something only those who have been there can truly grasp.

I learned the meaning of sacrifice --- not just the ultimate sacrifice of those who never made it home, but the daily sacrifices of every man (and today, women) who put their fears aside to do what was required. I learned to appreciate the minor comforts --- a letter from home, a quiet moment beneath the trees, the simple gift of another day.

And when I finally returned home, I carried those lessons with me. Vietnam taught me gratitude --- not just for surviving, but for truly living. For the freedom to wake up each morning without the weight of war on my shoulders. For the people I love and the time I have left. For the realization that every day is a gift, not to be wasted.

I don't romanticize that year nor dwell in its darkness. Instead, I hold onto the lessons --- strength, the perspective, the unbreakable bonds of brotherhood. Vietnam tested me, but it also shaped me. And for that, I am forever grateful.

2

RELATIONSHIPS

"At times, our light goes out and is rekindled by a spark from another person. Each of us has cause to think with deep gratitude of those who have lighted the flame within us."
— Albert Schweitzer.

"When we give cheerfully and accept gratefully, everyone is blessed."
— Maya Angelou.

We are family
I got all my sisters with me.
We are family
Get up, everybody, and sing.
We are family
I got all my sisters with me.
We are family
Get up, everybody, and sing.
—Sister Sledge.

What better way to start a relationship chapter than introducing Sister Sledge's *We Are Family*? It was released early in 1979 during a turbulent time. The United States was dealing with several domestic and foreign issues, including but not limited to the Iran hostage crisis, a nuclear power plant accident, and significant economic problems. It was a joyful song of unity and love. I have to feel that it significantly impacted the softening of the uncertain thoughts that many Americans carried with them.

In my case, my wife and I had just had a house built on Long Island. While we were getting settled, I always followed the Pittsburgh Pirates (my team at that time). Little did I know that

Sister Sledge's new song would be the spark that made the Pirates a cohesive unit founded on love and respect for each other.

We Are Family was the anthem of the 1979 Pittsburgh Pirates, symbolizing the team's unity and resilience. The song, initially recorded by Sister Sledge, became the team's rallying cry during their championship season. The Pirates, led by stars like Willie Stargell and Dave Parker, embraced the song's message of togetherness and perseverance, using it as motivation during their World Series run.

The phrase captured the spirit of a team that overcame adversity, including being down 3-1 in the World Series against the Baltimore Orioles before winning three straight games to clinch the title. The team's leader, Willie Stargell, was affectionately called "Pops" because of his mentorship and unifying presence. The Pirates' bond, on and off the field, made *We Are Family* a perfect representation of their championship journey.

To this day, *We Are Family* remains one of the most iconic team anthems in sports history.

The Pirate's experience demonstrates how gratitude plays a significant role in strengthening relationships. I want to introduce an article published in Psychology Today on June 1, 2020. The Greater Good Science Center at the University of California, Berkeley originally wrote it.

Do you have one person in your life for whom you feel grateful? Perhaps two or three people? How often might you say "thank you" to them for their actions or who they are? Expressing our appreciation for persons we are grateful for can strengthen our relationships in profound, meaningful, and rewarding ways.

Research shows that expressing gratitude for those we care about can improve the relationship for both parties by bringing us closer to the other individual and sustaining the relationship for the long term. If you need more convincing, here are five ways that relationships benefit by showing gratitude:

1. Expressing gratitude shows you care. When we show gratitude toward another in a relationship, we acknowledge a trait found in the other person. In the first study, psychologist Sara Algoe and researchers demonstrate that gratitude strengthens relationships: "Relationships with others who are responsive to our whole self --- our likes and dislikes, our needs and preferences --- can help us get through difficult times."

By showing responsiveness to our whole selves, expressing gratitude in and of itself shows we care for the recipient of that gratitude. Expressing gratitude is a powerful way of displaying affection; our relationships bring us closer together.

2. Expressing gratitude acknowledges a good deed by the other person. Professor of Psychology Barbara L. Frederickson describes gratitude as serving in part as a "moral barometer." In her book, The Psychology of Gratitude, she explains that gratitude "provides a reading of the moral significance of the situation" …and how the recipient of said gratitude acknowledges benefiting from a "moral action."

When we say "thank you" to another, we often respond with appreciation for this good deed, put another way. Our appreciative acknowledgment reveals an exchange of give and take. By serving as this "moral barometer," gratitude acknowledges benefiting from a "moral action."

3. Expressing gratitude reciprocates the kindness shared and felt in your relationship. In addition to responding to a good deed, expressing gratitude reciprocates kindness in our relationships. There is plenty to be said about kindness, too. After former NBA basketball star Kobe Bryant died in a tragic helicopter accident, scores of acquaintances hailed the

player's kindness off the court. By giving Bryant as an example, it is clear how sharing feelings of kindness in our relationships matters to both sides. So, why not share your appreciation for the individuals in your relationships? It can generate the kindness you might be missing.

4. Expressing gratitude celebrates the positivity in your relationship, bringing both sides closer together. When our relationships might be missing kindness or the muster we're looking for; gratitude can be a starting point for discovering the positive aspects of our connections. Celebrating good moments --- perhaps via an uplifting social media post or a hand-written thank-you note --- can help bring both sides closer together. When left unexpressed, our gratitude won't pay off in our relationships and eventually towards our well-being, even though we care deeply about this well-being.

5. Expressing gratitude makes us happy and satisfied and paves the way for future acts of kindness in the relationship. Robert Waldinger's 75-year study on adult development describes how our relationships are the most significant predictor of happiness and health. So, if gratitude can strengthen our relationships, then why not combine both potent ingredients (quality relationships and gratitude) toward gaining a more satisfying life? Daily considering our gratitude towards others can be a strong start to boosting our relationships, optimism, and mental health.

As we move forward from the works of Sister Sledge and the scientists at the University of California, Berkley, I would like to introduce a concept that correlates significantly with the power of gratitude. That is "mental subtraction."

There are moments in life when we find ourselves lost in dissatisfaction --- dwelling on what we lack, what has gone wrong, or what could be better. But what if we considered what could have been missing instead of focusing on what is missing? Mental subtraction is a simple yet profound practice: rather than counting our blessings, we imagine life without them. This shift in perspective can deepen our gratitude, intensify our appreciation, and remind us of the fragile beauty of what we have.

Imagine waking up one morning to find that something precious in your life --- your home, a loved one, your health --- had never existed. Not lost, not taken away, but never there to begin with.

What if you never met the person you love most?

What if you never had been given the opportunities that shaped your journey?

What if a slight twist of fate had led you down a completely different path --- one where the comforts and joys you take for granted were absent?

At first, this might seem unsettling, even painful. But that discomfort is precisely what makes mental subtraction so powerful. We learn to appreciate those things with renewed depth by imagining life without what we cherish.

Psychological studies confirm that mental subtraction enhances gratitude more effectively than simply listing things we're thankful for. A study published in The Journal of Personality and Social Psychology found that when participants were asked to imagine life without a positive event --- rather than simply reflecting on the event itself --- they reported significantly greater appreciation and life satisfaction. This practice works because our brains adapt quickly to blessings. Psychologists called this *"hedonic adaptation"* --- the tendency to get used to favorable circumstances, causing them to lose their impact over time. Mental subtraction disrupts this adaptation, making us see familiar joys with fresh eyes.

You don't need a crisis to practice mental subtraction. You can apply it in small, everyday ways.

- In Relationships: Instead of focusing on a loved one's flaws, imagine your life if you never met them. How different would the world be without their presence?
- In Career and Success: Rather than stressing over work frustrations, consider a version of your life where you never had the opportunities that led you here.
- In Health and Well-Being: On a tough day, instead of resenting aches, pains, or stress, reflect on a time when you were ill or injured. The mere ability to move, breathe, and experience life is a gift.

Mental subtraction doesn't require loss --- it simply invites us to pretend for a moment, just long enough to remind ourselves of what truly matters. When we do this, even mundane moments can be profound. The next time you sip coffee, hold a child's hand, or hear a familiar laugh, pause. Imagine if that experience had never been yours. Then, let gratitude settle in, more profound than before. Because sometimes, the best way to appreciate what we have is to imagine, just for a moment, what life would be without it.

The Bridge Out Of Loneliness: How Relationships Shape Our Sense Of Belonging

Loneliness is often misunderstood. It's not merely the absence of people; it's the absence of connection. One can be surrounded by crowds and still feel alone, just as another can sit in quiet solitude and feel deeply connected. What makes the difference? *Relationships.*

Human beings are wired for connection. From entering the world, we seek warmth, touch, and understanding. We are not meant to navigate life alone. Yet, deep, aching loneliness has become a silent epidemic, creeping into the lives of many, even in an age of constant communication.

Loneliness is not just an emotion but a burden on the soul. It distorts perception, making the world feel cooler, interactions feel shallower, and struggles feel heavier. It convinces us that we are unseen, unheard, and unimportant. Over time, loneliness erodes self-worth, leading to anxiety, depression, and even physical health issues. But the antidote to loneliness is not simply being around people --- it is fostering meaningful relationships.

When we form genuine connections --- with family, friends, romantic partners, or even a single kindred spirit --- we begin to rebuild the bridge out of loneliness. Relationships remind us that we matter, that our thoughts or feelings are valid, and that someone cares whether we wake up in the morning. A heartfelt conversation, a shared laugh, or a simple "How are you doing?" from someone who truly listens can make all the difference. In those moments, loneliness loses its grip.

The following are the role of relationships in combatting loneliness:

1. Friendship as a lifeline – A true friend doesn't just fill the silence; they understand it. Friendships provide a space where we can be ourselves without fear of judgment. Whether through deep conversations or lighthearted banter, a strong friendship can be a powerful shield against isolation.

2. Family as an anchor – While family dynamics can be complicated, they often provide a sense of belonging that nothing else can. A simple call from a sibling, a hug from a parent, or the shared history of growing up together can remind us that we are part of something bigger than ourselves.

3. Romantic love as a mirror – A loving partner reflects our worth, struggles, and joys. When healthy and nurturing, romantic relationships offer companionship in the truest

sense- someone to walk beside us, share burdens, and celebrate triumphs.

4. Community as a safety net – Sometimes, the cure for loneliness comes not from one deep connection but from a web of small, meaningful interactions. Being part of a group- whether a church, a volunteer organization, a book club, or even a group of coworkers helps reinforce our place in the world.

It is easy to believe that relationships should come to us and somebody should reach out if we are lonely. But the connection is a two-way street. Sometimes, breaking free from loneliness means taking the first step --- sending a message, making a call, and showing up when it's easier to stay in. When we do, we often find that others long for connection just as much as we do.

Loneliness can feel like an endless void, but relationships are the light that guide us out. Through deep bonds or simple, everyday interactions, human connection can heal, uplift, and remind us that we are never truly alone. Because, in the end, life is not meant to be lived in isolation. It is intended to be shared.

In my book, "Citizen Can," I introduced a concept where the activities of human beings correlate to those of cells in the human body. I believe it is essential to present this concept here. If we looked at our thoughts and activities in the context of how our cells operate, we would better understand the importance of a positive approach to our relationships with others.

Human Beings: The Cells Of Humanity

Imagine the human body --- an intricate, self-sustaining system where millions of cells work harmoniously. Each cell has a purpose and a role to play, and though different in function, they all contribute to the greater whole. In many ways, human beings are just like these cells, each of us a vital part of the vast organism that is humanity.

Consider the heart cells --- constantly working, pumping life throughout the body. They resemble the caregivers, the leaders, the ones who pour love and energy into our communities, keeping the world moving forward.

Then there are the neurons, sending signals and ideas, much like teachers, innovators, and visionaries who shape our collective knowledge and progress. Without them, our society would lack direction and wisdom.

Some people are like immune cells, tirelessly fighting to protect others --- doctors, activists, and first responders, always ready to defend against harm and heal those in need.

Even the smallest, most overlooked cells --- like those in the skin --- play a crucial role, just as the everyday workers, parents, and quiet helpers provide protection, warmth, and a sense of belonging.

But what happens when cells refuse to work together? When they compete rather than collaborate? Disease takes hold --- just as a society, when selfishness, division, and greed threaten the collective well-being. Like cancerous cells, unchecked negativity can spread, disrupting the balance of our shared existence. However, when the cells act as they should --- communicating, supporting one another, and recognizing their role in the bigger picture --- the body survives. And so does humanity.

No matter how small we feel, we have a role to play. When we work in unity, appreciating our differences yet embracing our shared purpose, we create something greater than ourselves --- a world that is healthy, strong, and full of life.

Just like the cells in a body, we are not meant to work alone. We are meant to work together.

I want to conclude the discussion on relationships by sharing two firsthand experiences showing me the power of positive connections in strengthening our society. My years of involvement with the Boys & Girls Clubs and Sterling Estates Senior Services Center have demonstrated how these institutions serve as bookends, providing support at both ends of life's journey. Together, they create opportunities for individuals to thrive—whether in their formative years, during advanced education, or throughout their professional lives.

Together, these two institutions act as stabilizing forces in society. Boys & Girls Clubs nurture the future, while senior centers honor the past. When communities support both young and old, they create a more compassionate, knowledgeable, and resilient society where every generation has purpose and value.

My 13 years as an executive at the Boys & Girls Club of Metro Atlanta showed me why it is considered a positive place for kids. Boys & Girls Clubs play a crucial role in communities by providing a safe and supportive environment for children and teens to learn, grow, and build essential life skills. Here's why Boys & Girls Clubs are so important:

1. **Safe and Positive Environment** – They offer a secure place where kids can go after school, reducing the risk of engaging in unsafe activities or being left unsupervised.
2. **Academic Support** – Many clubs provide homework help, tutoring, and access to technology, helping kids succeed in school and prepare for future careers.
3. **Character and Leadership Development** – Programs encourage kids to become responsible, caring citizens through volunteer opportunities and leadership training.
4. **Healthy Lifestyles** – Clubs promote physical fitness, nutrition education, and mental wellness, helping kids develop healthy habits.

5. **Social and Emotional Growth** – Children build friendships, gain confidence, and learn critical social skills that prepare them for adulthood.
6. **Affordable and Accessible** – Many families rely on the Clubs because they provide high-quality programs at little to no cost, making them accessible to those who need them most.
7. **Positive Role Models** – Staff and mentors provide guidance, encouragement, and support, helping kids navigate challenges and set future goals.

Overall, Boys & Girls Clubs strengthen communities by investing in young people, empowering them to reach their full potential. Have you had any personal experience with a Boys & Girls Club?

About 15 years after retiring from the Boys & Girls Clubs of Metro Atlanta, I had the opportunity to volunteer at Sterling Estates, an upscale senior living facility. This experience showed firsthand how these two organizations are vital in supporting society at both ends of life's journey. Sterling Estates participates to enhance our journey in the following manner:

Sterling Estates is a vital hub for older adults, promoting independence, well-being, and community engagement. Its purpose extends beyond providing essential services—it enriches lives, fosters social connections, and enhances overall quality of life.

Purpose of a Senior Citizen Center

1. Social Connection & Engagement – Reduces isolation by offering a welcoming space for seniors to interact, build friendships, and stay involved in their communities.
2. Health & Wellness – Provides physical fitness programs, nutrition services, and mental health resources to support a healthy lifestyle.

3. Lifelong Learning – Encourages continued personal growth through educational classes, workshops, and skill-building opportunities.
4. Support Services – Assists with transportation, financial planning, healthcare navigation, and other essential resources to maintain independence.
5. Intergenerational Impact – Bridges the gap between generations by fostering mentorship, volunteering, and shared experiences with younger individuals.

The Power Of A Senior Citizen Center

A well-run center empowers older adults by keeping them active, engaged, and purposeful. It transforms aging from a decline stage into a time of growth and contribution, ensuring that seniors remain valued, connected, and supported within society. Ultimately, it strengthens the entire community by honoring the experience and wisdom of its elders.

During my three years of volunteering at Sterling Estates, I took on several activities that I believe added to the growth and fun of the residents. I know it did for me. I was involved in activities such as bingo, bridge, and trivia, lectured at their breakfast club, and even taught poker. However, the activity that I know was most rewarding was a weekly discussion on current events. I was allowed to create my agenda for the debate. I included the following:

1. Uplifting quote of the day
2. A word of the day
3. Events that happened on that day in history
4. Famous people who were born on that day
5. Famous people who died on that day
6. Led a discussion about current news topics
7. I finished with a few trivia questions. *They loved that part.*

As the word spread around the center, more and more residents came to the session. We had a lot of fun, but unfortunately, it was brought to a halt by COVID-19.

The most fulfilling aspect for me was the friendships I formed, many of which I have endured. After COVID-19 faded, I stayed in touch with some residents through Zoom calls, provided they were comfortable with the technology. We reminisced about our experiences from the live sessions during these virtual meetings. Over time, I began meeting some of them for coffee gatherings and breakfasts, deepening our connections. I also formed a close bond with a wonderful friend who later became my bridge partner for several years.

To conclude this chapter, I want it understood that gratitude is not just a feeling --- it is a practice, a habit, and a choice. Cultivating gratitude in our relationships creates deeper connections, reduces conflict, and strengthens the bonds that matter most. By making gratitude a daily part of interacting with others, we nurture love, trust, and joy.

Ultimately, relationships that thrive are not those free of hardships but those where gratitude is woven into the fabric of love and connection.

Don't forget how *Love and The Golden Rule* are critical to the connections between relationships and gratitude.

3

ACCOMPLISHMENTS

"Appreciation is a wonderful thing. It makes what is excellent in others belong to us as well."
—Voltaire

"No matter what accomplishments you make, somebody helped you."
—Althea Gibson

"Great things can happen when you don't care who gets the credit."
—Mark Twain

Gratitude is often regarded as a personal virtue, a simple act of appreciation for what one has. However, its impact extends far beyond mere politeness or social etiquette. Research and anecdotal evidence suggest that gratitude plays a significant role in shaping an individual's accomplishments. This chapter explores how gratitude fosters success, resilience, and motivation, ultimately leading to more extraordinary achievements in various aspects of life.

Gratitude has a profound effect on the human mind. Psychological studies show that regularly practicing gratitude enhances positive emotions, reduces stress, and strengthens well-being. When individuals acknowledge and appreciate their progress, they cultivate a growth-oriented mindset crucial for achieving long-term goals. A grateful mindset helps in:

- Enhancing self-confidence: Recognizing past achievements boosts self-esteem and encourages individuals to take on more significant challenges.

- Reducing fear of failure: Acknowledging past successes and the support received from others fosters resilience, making individuals more likely to persevere through setbacks.
- Strengthening motivation: Expressing gratitude for opportunities fuels intrinsic motivation, leading to increased effort and productivity.

Success is not solely dependent on talent or hard work; mindset plays a pivotal role. Gratitude fosters a perspective that helps stay committed to their goals. People who appreciate the journey rather than solely focusing on the destination remain engaged, persistent, and driven. Ways gratitude contributes to goal achievement:

- Increased perseverance: Those who practice gratitude regularly are more likely to remain committed to long-term goals, as they find joy in the process rather than just the outcome.
- Better decision-making: Gratitude encourages a balanced outlook, allowing individuals to make thoughtful and informed choices.
- Stronger social connections: Expressing gratitude strengthens relationships with mentors, peers, and supporters, creating a network that facilitates success.

Gratitude has a direct correlation with productivity. Employees and professionals who feel appreciated and who practice gratitude are more engaged, satisfied, and productive. Organizations that cultivate a culture of gratitude experience higher levels of teamwork, morale, and overall performance. Benefits of gratitude in professional settings include:

- Higher engagement: Employees who feel valued are more committed to their work.
- Better leadership: Leaders who express gratitude foster loyalty and motivation among team members.

- Enhanced creativity: A grateful mindset reduces stress, allowing for more incredible innovation and problem-solving skills.

To harness the benefits of gratitude, individuals must actively incorporate it into their daily lives. Here are some effective strategies:

- Keeping a gratitude journal: This was mentioned in Chapter One but can't stressed enough. Writing down daily accomplishments and things to be grateful for reinforces a positive mindset.
- Expressing appreciation: Verbally or in writing, acknowledging the contributions of others strengthens relationships and builds a supportive environment.
- Practicing mindfulness: Being present and appreciating small wins leads to sustained motivation.
- Reframing setbacks: Viewing challenges as learning opportunities rather than failure fosters resilience and continuous improvement.

At this moment, I would like to share two articles that further highlight the significance of gratitude in achieving success. The first was on January 21, 2025, entitled "Embracing Accomplishments: A New Year's Perspective". Elizabeth DuPont Spencer LCSW-C wrote it. She is a licensed clinical social worker and board-approved supervisor with 30 years of experience in private practice. The Anxiety & Depression Association of America presented the article.

As we welcome a new year, it's common for us to set resolutions and goals for the months ahead. While looking towards the future is important, it's equally important to take a moment to reflect on the past year and appreciate our accomplishments. Often, we are so focused on what we want to achieve next that we forget to celebrate how far we've come. The beginning of a new year is the perfect time to pause and embrace our accomplishments, using them as a source of motivation and inspiration for the journey ahead. In this blog post, we will discuss the importance of taking a moment to appreciate our achievements and how they can positively impact our mindset for the new year.

Appreciating the Journey in the Rearview Mirror

Reflecting on the past year can often draw our focus towards what wasn't achieved. It's a common tendency but not one that always serves us well. Instead, we ought to pivot our viewpoint, giving due recognition to the journey we've embarked on. Both our personal and professional paths have merit and are deserving of our admiration.

Consider the grit and resilience you have shown over the year. Every challenging situation you navigated, every late-night consultation you offered, each difficult conversation you steered—all are pieces of evidence of your dedication and persistence. Now, let's not forget about the clients whose lives you've touched and made a difference in. The mental health milestones they achieved with your help and the obstacles they overcame—are they not victories worth savoring?

It's often the little things, the small wins, that make a big difference. They might not seem significant in isolation, but collectively, they add up to a journey of transformation. The clients you've counseled, the knowledge you've gained, the personal growth you've experienced – these are not insignificant achievements. They are the very fabric of your professional evolution.

So, as we glance back, let's not let unmet goals cloud our perspective. Instead, let's acknowledge and relish the victories, regardless of their size. Each one of them is a piece of the puzzle that fits into the larger picture of who we are as professionals. We've come a long way, and this journey, with its peaks and valleys, has shaped us, molded us, and made us better mental health professionals. So, here's to celebrating our journey and appreciating the path that's led us here.

Celebrating Personal and Professional Growth

Every revolution around the sun brings with it a plethora of unique experiences that foster our growth, both on a personal and professional level. Reflect on the distinct ways you have expanded your horizons in the past year. Perhaps your empathetic understanding deepened, patience tested and fortified, or your toolkit of therapeutic skills broadened. Maybe your success stretched beyond personal growth, manifesting in the lives of your clients as they navigated and triumphed over their mental health challenges under your guidance. Or perhaps it was the expansion of your practice that marked your growth. Each of these developments, irrespective of their scale, are indeed worth rejoicing over. They are tangible markers of your evolution as a mental health professional, evidence of how you dared to transcend the bounds of your comfort zone and grew beyond what you were.

Embracing Accomplishments as Fuel for the Future

Dwelling on missed marks can often eclipse our actual accomplishments. But imagine if, instead, we allowed our achievements to shine through as a beacon for our future? Each victory, no matter how small, speaks volumes about our resilience and commitment to the cause. It serves as a gentle nudge, reminding us of the immense potential that lies within us. As we stand on the threshold of a brand-new year, let's pledge to use our past accomplishments not just as reminders of what we've achieved but as the propellers driving us toward new milestones.

Our achievements are a testament to our ability to rise to the occasion, confront challenges, and prevail. They are undeniable proof of our capacity to make a difference in the lives of those we serve. With each accomplishment, we not only make strides in our professional growth, but we also inspire hope and resilience in our clients, empowering them on their path to mental wellness.

As we stride into the uncharted territories of the new year, let's allow these accomplishments to motivate and energize us. Let's let them serve as our compass, guiding us through the complexities of our profession, reminding us of our unwavering determination, and fueling our aspirations.

So, here's to embracing the past as we pave the path for the future. Here's to allowing our victories, triumphs, and accomplishments to serve as the bedrock for our continued growth. As we look ahead, let's not forget to glance back from time to time, drawing strength from our achievements and using them as a catalyst, propelling us forward into the new year and beyond.

The Power of Positive Affirmation

Unleashing the strength of positive affirmations, we step into an empowering space that bolsters our self-perception and fortifies our conviction in our capabilities. When we actively engage in affirming our accomplishments, it's far from a simple self-congratulatory pat on the back. Instead, it's an act of anchoring our self-esteem and cultivating our confidence, underpinning the firm belief that we can confront and conquer future challenges with resilience. With the dawn of the new year, let's immerse ourselves in the practice of positive affirmations. These affirmations will reverberate within us as constant reminders of our worth and potential, solidifying our resolve to approach future goals with determination.

Cultivating Gratitude

Amid the bustling rhythm of our work as mental health providers, it's easy to overlook the simple yet powerful practice of gratitude. But pause for a moment, and you'll realize that gratitude has a significant role to play in our professional lives. It's an opportunity for us to give thanks for the progress we've made, the lessons we've learned, and the strength we've built over the past year. The act of being thankful for our accomplishments fosters a positive mindset, sparking an inner light that can guide us through the challenges of our profession.

When we cultivate gratitude, we are not just acknowledging our achievements. We're also recognizing the invaluable support that we've received from those around us. Our colleagues who've shared their wisdom and experience, mentors who've guided us through the intricate maze of mental health practice, and our clients who've trusted us with their vulnerabilities — they all deserve our heartfelt appreciation.

Reflecting on our past year, let's weave gratitude into the very fabric of our introspection. By doing so, we nurture a culture of appreciation within our professional circles and within ourselves. It is an act of kindness, a gesture of humility, a gentle reminder of our interconnectedness. It affirms that our successes are not solitary feats but collective victories.

And remember, gratitude does more than just enhance our professional wellbeing. It equips us with a lens of positivity, enabling us to perceive our experiences through an optimistic prism. It softens the edges of our challenges, highlighting the silver linings and uncovering hidden opportunities. It fuels our enthusiasm, preparing us to embrace the new year with a hopeful heart and a resilient spirit.

So, let's make room for gratitude. Let's give thanks for the year that's passed, for the paths we've trodden, the heights we've scaled, and the growth we've experienced. Because in gratitude, we find the strength to continue our journey, to meet the new year head-on, and to continue making a difference in the lives of those we serve.

The second article I will present is from an organization called "Career Guidance Advice." CGA is a premier online directory connecting individuals with expert career guidance advisors. It appeared on December 19, 2023.

Success is worth celebrating! Whether it's reaching a personal goal, completing a challenging project, or earning recognition at work, acknowledging your achievements fuels growth and confidence. As priorities shift and new challenges arise, taking the time to reflect on your wins is more important than ever. This article dives into the value of celebrating your achievements, creative ways to recognize success, and tips to keep that positive momentum going.

The Value Of Celebrating Your Achievements

Acknowledging success isn't just about feeling good – it builds self-confidence, inspires others, and keeps you motivated for the future. As we move into a new year, the pace of life often leads to overlooking personal victories, but pausing to recognize progress helps to:

- *Boost self-esteem and reinforce your ability to achieve goals.*
- *Create lasting memories tied to your hard work and dedication.*
- *Strengthen relationships by sharing successes with others.*

Celebration fosters gratitude and positivity, counteracting the stress of modern life.

Identifying Your Achievements

When life gets busy, it's easy to forget how much you've accomplished. Start by:

- *Reflecting on the past year and noting key milestones.*
- *Ask yourself, "What did I overcome?" and "What made me proud?"*
- *Including both big achievements (promotions, awards) and small wins (meeting deadlines, learning new skills).*

For a structured approach, try keeping a "success journal" or a "brag book," where you jot down weekly or monthly wins. This habit helps maintain perspective and reinforces a mindset of gratitude.

Creative Ways To Celebrate Your Achievements

Celebrations don't have to be extravagant. Here are a few ideas:

- *Personal Rewards: Treat yourself to something meaningful, such as a dinner out, a spa day, or that gadget you've been eyeing.*
- *Memorializing Milestones: Create a photo book, scrapbook, or framed certificate to mark the moment.*

- *Share with Loved Ones: Host a small gathering, write a thank-you note to those who supported you, or simply share your joy on social media.*
- *Take a Break: A day off to recharge can be the ultimate reward.*
- *Charity or Giving Back: Celebrate by donating to a cause you care about, linking your success to helping others.*

The key is choosing something that feels authentic and fulfilling for you.

The Role Of Recognition In Motivation

Rewarding success isn't just an acknowledgment of the past; it's also an investment in the future. Here's why:

- *Encouraging Consistency: Celebrations reinforce behaviors that lead to success.*
- *Boosting Morale: Tangible rewards, even small ones, make the effort feel worthwhile.*
- *Cultivating Resilience: Recognizing past wins helps you tackle new challenges with confidence.*

In workplaces, recognition programs have been shown to improve employee satisfaction, retention, and productivity. The same principles apply to personal life.

Building A Culture Of Celebration In The Workplace

In 2025 and beyond, creating a culture that values achievements is essential for employee engagement. Here's how:

- *Frequent Recognition: Celebrate team wins in meetings, newsletters, or events.*
- *Personalized Rewards: Tailor rewards to individual preferences for maximum impact.*
- *Incorporate Feedback: Allow team members to nominate peers for recognition.*

- *Celebrate Progress, Not Just Results: Acknowledge milestones reached during long-term projects.*

By fostering an environment of appreciation, organizations can boost collaboration, innovation, and morale.

Challenges In Celebrating Your Achievements

Despite its benefits, celebrating your achievements isn't always easy. Common barriers include:

- *Self-Doubt: Feeling like your accomplishments aren't "big enough" to celebrate.*
- *Cultural Factors: Some cultures emphasize humility over self-recognition.*
- *Workplace Norms: High-pressure environments may prioritize productivity over acknowledgment.*

To overcome these, focus on the value of recognition for yourself and others. Celebrations needn't be grand — they simply need to be genuine.

Tips For Maintaining A Positive Momentum

Celebrating success is only the beginning. To build on that energy:

- *Set New Goals: Use your achievements as a springboard for future ambitions.*
- *Reflect Regularly: Make reflection a monthly habit to stay aware of progress.*
- *Seek Feedback: Asking for constructive input keeps you growing while celebrating what's going well.*
- *Surround Yourself with Positivity: Engage with communities that uplift and inspire you.*

Momentum thrives on a combination of gratitude, goal-setting, and a supportive environment.

Conclusion

Celebrating your achievements is a cornerstone of personal and professional growth. Whether you're recognizing your progress or fostering a culture of acknowledgment at work, celebrating fuels motivation, confidence, and resilience. In 2024, make it a priority to reflect on and reward successes- big and small. Remember, every step forward is worth cherishing!

I want to wrap up this discussion on the influence of gratitude in sync with personal achievements by sharing two experiences that reinforce this idea.

The Gift Of Gratitude: My Journey With *Citizen Can*

I felt excitement and fear the first time I stared at the blank page. Writing a book had always been a distant dream, something I admired in others but never truly believed I could accomplish. Yet, as I began writing *Citizen Can*, I had no idea that beyond the words, chapters, and late nights, I would understand one of life's greatest lessons—gratitude.

In the beginning, the process was exhilarating. I poured my thoughts onto the page, shaping ideas and narratives that had long lived in my mind. But soon, the reality of writing a book set in. Doubt crept in. Was my story worth telling? Would anyone care? There were moments when I felt stuck, overwhelmed by the enormity of the task. However, in those moments of uncertainty, I discovered the power of gratitude.

I found gratitude in the encouragement of friends who listened patiently as I rambled about my ideas. I found it in the mentors who guided me, offering constructive feedback that helped shape my writing. Even in my struggles—writer's block, self-doubt, exhaustion—I began to recognize the value of the journey. The long nights of editing, the rewrites, and the rejections weren't just obstacles; they were steppingstones, each teaching me patience, resilience, and appreciation for the process.

Then came the moment I held *Citizen Can* in my hands for the first time. The feeling was indescribable—pride, relief, and an overwhelming sense of gratitude. But the real reward came later. A reader reached out to me, sharing how my book resonated with them and somehow shifted their perspective. That was when I truly understood the impact of my work—not just as a personal accomplishment but as something meaningful to others.

Writing *Citizen Can* didn't just fulfill a dream; it changed me. It opened my eyes to the importance of gratitude—not just for the outcome, but for every challenge, every lesson, and every person who played a role in my journey. I learned that success isn't just about reaching the finish line; it's about appreciating the path that leads you there.

And for that, I am forever grateful.

A Journey Of Gratitude: 34 Years Of Sobriety

There was a time when I couldn't imagine a life without alcohol. It was my escape, my coping mechanism, and, for far too long, my identity. What started as social drinking slowly became something else—a crutch, a shadow that followed me everywhere. I realized something had to change when I found myself at the lowest point of my life, staring at the consequences of my choices.

Admitting I needed help was one of the hardest things I've ever done. I was afraid—afraid of who I'd be without alcohol, afraid of facing the pain I had been numbing for so long. But that moment of surrender led me to a six-week stay at a recovery clinic, a decision that saved my life.

Rehab was grueling. The days included therapy, reflection, and painful honesty. I had to confront the reasons behind my drinking, the emotions I had buried, and the relationships I had strained. But as difficult as it was, I found something unexpected—hope. The counselors, my fellow patients, and the program's routine gave me structure and a sense of purpose. I felt like I was reclaiming myself for the first time in years.

After rehab, I knew my journey wasn't over. Recovery wasn't just about quitting alcohol; it was about rebuilding my life. That's when I walked through the doors of Alcoholics Anonymous. At first, I wasn't sure if I belonged there. But as I listened to others share their stories—their struggles, victories, and setbacks—I realized I wasn't alone. AA became my refuge, where I could be honest without fear of judgment. The 12-step program gave me not just the tools to stay sober but the foundation to live with purpose, accountability, and, most importantly, gratitude.

Yet, none of this would have been possible without the unwavering support of my family and friends. They stood by me, even when I didn't deserve it. They forgave me, even when I struggled to forgive myself. They reminded me, time and again, that I was worth saving. Their love nurtured my recovery, giving me the strength to keep going, even on the most challenging days.

Now, 34 years later, I look back with pride and deep gratitude. I am grateful for the struggle because it made me stronger. I am thankful for the people who lifted me when I couldn't stand on my own. I am grateful every day I wake up sober, knowing I was given another chance to live fully, love deeply, and give back to those who need the same hope I once sought.

Sobriety is not just about not drinking. It is about gratitude—for the journey, the lessons, and the people who walked beside me every step of the way.

And for that, I am forever grateful.

4

TEACHING GRATITUDE TO OTHERS: PAYING FORWARD

"You can't live a perfect day without doing something for someone who will never be able to repay you."
— John Wooden.

"The best way to find yourself is to lose yourself in the service of others."
— Mahatma Gandhi.

"I have come to believe that a great teacher is a great artist and that there are as few as there are any other great artists. Teaching might even be the greatest of the arts since the medium is the human mind and spirit."
— John Steinbeck.

"It is only as we develop others that we permanently succeed."
— Harry S. Firestone.

I believe Mahatma Gandhi's lifelong pursuit of peace is a powerful way to begin this chapter, highlighting how he embraced gratitude as an essential tool in his journey.

His journey began when he embraced the dusty roads of South Africa, which stretched endlessly before Mohandas Karamchand Gandhi as he walked toward the Pietermaritzburg railway station. His heart still pounded from the humiliation of being thrown off the first-class train compartment for being an Indian despite holding a valid ticket. He could have let anger consume him. He could have chosen revenge. But instead, he decided something different --- he chose gratitude.

As he sat in the cold station that night, wrapped in his thoughts, he realized that this moment of injustice was not a curse but a blessing in disguise. It was a lesson, a calling to awaken himself and an entire people. He silently gave thanks ---not for the pain, but for the opportunity it presented. This gratitude transformed his outrage into a lifelong pursuit of peace and justice.

Gratitude As Strength In Adversity

Throughout his life, Gandhi faced opposition, imprisonment, and violence. Yet, he consistently responded not with bitterness but with gratitude. Gandhi did not dwell on his suffering when jailed for his protests against British rule in India. Instead, he saw his time in prison as an opportunity to reflect, write, and strengthen his commitment to nonviolence.

One of his prison guards once asked him, "Why do you not curse those who put you here?"

Gandhi smiled and replied, *"I am grateful for every challenge; it teaches patience and fortitude. Without struggle, how would I learn resilience?"*

This simple philosophy allowed him to turn suffering into wisdom and oppression into motivation. He did not waste energy on hatred; instead, he channeled his gratitude into action, making every hardship a steppingstone toward peace.

Gratitude Towards His Oppressors

Perhaps one of the most profound ways Gandhi demonstrated gratitude was in his relationship with his adversaries. Whether it was the British rulers or those who opposed his philosophy of nonviolence, he never let resentment dictate his actions. He was known to say, *"The best way to find yourself is to lose yourself in the service of others."*

He even expressed appreciation for the British in his writings, not because he agreed with their rule but because their presence had awakened a sense of unity among Indians. He believed their resistance gave India a purpose—to reclaim its independence through truth and nonviolence.

When India finally gained independence in 1947, many expected Gandhi to revel in victory. Instead, he reminded his followers to show gratitude even to their former rulers, for it was through their struggle that the nation had found its strength.

Gratitude As A Tool For Peace

Gandhi's gratitude extended beyond his personal experiences; he used it to unite people in times of division. When religious violence broke out between Hindus and Muslims during the partition of India, Gandhi, despite his frail health, traveled from village to village, urging people to forgive and embrace each other.

One evening, a grief-stricken man approached him, confessing that he had killed a Muslim child in revenge for the murder of his son. The man's hands trembled, his eyes pleading for redemption.

Gandhi, weak from fasting, whispered, *"Find an orphaned Muslim boy. Raise him as your own. Teach him love, not hatred. And be grateful for the chance to make amends."*

The man wept, not expecting such wisdom, but he knew at that moment that gratitude had the power to heal even the deepest wounds.

The Legacy Of Gratitude

Mahatma Gandhi's life was a testament to the transformative power of gratitude. He did not see gratitude as passive acceptance but as an active force that turned adversity into purpose, enemies into friends, and suffering into strength. He understood that true peace could never be achieved through vengeance but only through a heart that recognized the value of every experience—good or bad.

His influence stretched beyond India, inspiring leaders like Martin Luther King Jr. and Nelson Mandela, who embraced gratitude to foster peace. His legacy remains a reminder that gratitude can illuminate the path to justice and harmony, even in the face of the greatest struggles.

Even today, his words echo through time:

> *"A grateful heart is a peaceful heart. And a peaceful heart is the foundation of a peaceful world."*

Gratitude is vital in utilizing your gifts to benefit others by paying your blessings forward. Let's examine how gratitude plays a crucial role in children's education.

Gratitude is a transformative force in education, shaping the teacher's approach and the student's ability to learn and grow. When teaching --- especially children --- gratitude fosters a positive environment where encouragement, empathy, and appreciation thrive. It goes beyond a simple "thank you"; it is an attitude that nurtures respect, enhances motivation, and strengthens relationships.

Gratitude As A Foundation For Teaching

A teacher's attitude significantly impacts a child's learning experience. When educators approach teaching with gratitude, they cultivate patience, resilience, and a sense of purpose. Instead of viewing challenges as burdens, they see them as opportunities to help children grow. A teacher who is grateful for the chance to shape young minds instills the same mindset in students.

For instance, a teacher who expresses appreciation for a student's efforts—no matter how small—encourages perseverance. Children who struggle with math but receive recognition for their attempts rather than their successes learn to value effort, fostering a growth mindset, where mistakes are seen as steppingstones rather than failures.

Modeling Gratitude For Children

Children learn best by example. When teachers and parents consistently express gratitude, children internalize this behavior. Simple actions, like thanking a student for their participation or recognizing acts of kindness in the classroom, reinforce the importance of appreciation.

By saying, *"I'm grateful for the way you helped your classmate today"* or *"Thank you for your patience while I explain this concept,"* educators teach children that gratitude is not just a reaction but a proactive way to strengthen relationships. Over time, children mirror this behavior, leading to a more supportive and empathetic learning environment.

Gratitude And Emotional Intelligence

Teaching gratitude enhances emotional intelligence in children, helping them navigate social interactions with kindness and understanding. Grateful children are likelier to show empathy, regulate emotions, and engage positively with others. When students recognize the efforts of their teachers, parents, and peers, they develop a sense of responsibility and community.

A classroom where gratitude is practiced fosters cooperation rather than competition. Children who appreciate one another's strengths and efforts create a culture of mutual respect, making learning more enjoyable and inclusive.

The Long-Term Impact Of Teaching Gratitude

Gratitude is a skill that extends far beyond childhood. Children who grow up with an attitude of appreciation are more likely to develop resilience, maintain strong relationships, and approach challenges with optimism. They carry these lessons into adulthood, becoming individuals who uplift and inspire others.

By integrating gratitude into education, we do more than teach children academic lessons—we equip them with a mindset that enhances their well-being, relationships, and overall success. In teaching gratitude, we nurture compassionate, mindful, and responsible individuals who understand the value of appreciation and kindness.

Beyond its impact on teaching children, gratitude also lays the foundation for ongoing acts of kindness, inspiring individuals to pay their gifts forward in adulthood.

Gratitude is more than an emotion --- it is a powerful force that inspires action, strengthens connections, and fosters generosity. When people experience genuine appreciation, they are more inclined to give back, creating a cycle of kindness far beyond the initial act. This is particularly significant when considering how gratitude influences how we pay forward gifts to adults and senior citizens.

Paying it forward is rooted in the understanding that kindness is not meant to end with us; instead, it is a gift to be shared. When individuals acknowledge the blessings in their lives, they naturally desire to extend them to others, especially those who have contributed wisdom, care, and guidance—like elders in our communities.

Gratitude As A Catalyst For Generosity

Gratitude shifts our perspective from scarcity to abundance. When people recognize and appreciate what they have, they are more likely to share their time, resources, and kindness. This generosity is particularly impactful when directed toward adults and seniors, who often face challenges such as loneliness, financial strain, or health issues.

For example, an adult who recalls their parents' or mentors' sacrifices may feel compelled to give back meaningfully --- through simple gestures like regular phone calls or more significant acts like assisting with daily errands. A community member who appreciates the support they once received may decide to pay it forward by volunteering at a senior center or donating to programs that benefit the elderly.

The Emotional Power Of Paying It Forward

Expressing gratitude through giving is not just beneficial for the receiver—it also enhances the giver's well-being. Studies have shown that acts of generosity increase feelings of happiness, reduce stress, and create a sense of fulfillment. When gratitude drives these actions, they become even more meaningful.

For adults and senior citizens, receiving kindness often has a profound emotional impact. Many older individuals have spent their lives giving—whether as parents, mentors, or caregivers. As they age, they may feel forgotten or undervalued. When someone acknowledges their contributions and pays kindness forward, it reaffirms their worth. It reminds them that they are still an integral part of the community.

Ways To Pay Gratitude Forward To Adults And Seniors

There are countless ways to express gratitude by giving back, and even small actions can make a significant difference. Here are some meaningful ways to pay it forward:

- Personal Acts of Appreciation: Taking time to write a heartfelt note, make a phone call, or visit an elderly neighbor shows gratitude in a profoundly personal way.
- Sharing Knowledge and Skills: Adults and seniors have a wealth of experience, and acknowledging their wisdom by asking for advice or learning from them can be an empowering exchange.

- Acts of Service: Helping with daily tasks—such as grocery shopping, home repairs, or technology assistance—demonstrates appreciation in a practical and impactful manner.
- Creating Opportunities for Connection: Organizing community events, offering transportation to social gatherings, or engaging in meaningful conversations can reduce feelings of isolation for senior citizens.
- Financial and Charitable Support: Donating to organizations that support the elderly, funding meals for those in need, or contributing to healthcare initiatives can create lasting change.

The Legacy Of Gratitude And Giving

When gratitude fuels paying it forward, it creates a lasting legacy of kindness. The beauty of this cycle is that generosity often inspires more generosity. A senior citizen who receives an act of kindness may, in turn, share their wisdom, encouragement, or resources with someone else. An adult who experiences gratitude-driven generosity may be motivated to continue the chain of giving, ensuring that appreciation and kindness spread through generations.

Ultimately, gratitude is a bridge that connects people across age groups, fostering a culture of respect, care, and mutual support. By embracing gratitude as a guiding principle, we enrich our lives and create a world where kindness is continually passed forward—especially to those who have paved the way before us.

A Grateful Journey: How Fordham University Shaped My Life

Standing at the gates of Fordham University, I couldn't help but feel a mix of emotions --- hope, uncertainty, and an overwhelming sense of gratitude. My journey to this moment had been anything but ordinary. Returning from my service in Vietnam, I carried experiences that had shaped me in ways I never imagined. Yet, as I transitioned back to civilian life, I found myself searching for direction, for a place where I could build my future.

Fordham took a chance on me. They saw a veteran and a student eager to learn and grow. They believed in me when I wasn't sure if I could believe in myself. That acceptance was more than just an admission letter --- it was an opportunity, a fresh start. For that, I have always been grateful.

Lessons In Diligence And Hard Work

From my first semester, Fordham taught me the value of diligence and discipline. The structure of military life instilled in me a sense of responsibility. Still, the college presented a new challenge that required focus, perseverance, and the ability to adapt. My professors pushed me to apply myself, to not just go through the motions but to engage with my studies truly.

I quickly learned that success wasn't about being the most intelligent person in the room but dedication. Late nights spent studying, countless hours in the library, and moments of self-doubt eventually gave way to a more profound confidence. Fordham nurtured an appreciation for hard work, showing me I could accomplish more than I ever thought possible with effort and determination.

A Pivotal Change: From Marketing To Accounting

When I first arrived, I intended to major in marketing. It seemed like a logical choice --- business-oriented and practical. But as I progressed through my courses, I was drawn to something else: accounting. It was a field that required precision, problem-solving, and meticulous attention to detail --- qualities I had honed in the military.

The encouragement of my professors and mentors at Fordham gave me the confidence to make the switch. They saw potential in me before I saw it in myself. Changing my major to accounting was one of the best decisions I ever made. It opened doors to a career I hadn't initially considered, but I soon realized it was where I belonged.

A Career Sparked By Opportunity

Fordham's impact didn't stop in the classroom. The university's strong alumni network proved one of its greatest gifts. Through their connections, I was introduced to a prominent alumnus who saw my potential and took a chance on me, just as Fordham had. That introduction led to my first job in accounting, setting me on a path that would shape the rest of my professional life.

Looking back, I often think about how different my life might have been had I not chosen Fordham or had Fordham not chosen me. The education, the mentorship, the network, not to mention the opportunity to meet my lifelong partner, Nena, played a crucial role in my journey. But more than anything, this institution's belief in me made all the difference.

Today, I carry the lessons of diligence, perseverance, and gratitude—lessons Fordham instilled in me from the beginning. I am forever grateful for the chance they took, the guidance they provided, and the opportunities they created. My story is one of transformation, and Fordham was the foundation that made it all possible.

A Grateful Heart: The Gift Of The Unchuan Family

When I married my wife, I gained more than just a life partner --- I became part of a family that would forever shape my life in ways I never expected. The Unchuans welcomed me with open arms, not as an outsider but as one of their own. From the beginning, I felt the depth of their warmth, unwavering love, and the deep-rooted values they carried that have left a lasting imprint on my heart.

Acceptance And Love: The Foundation Of Family

The Unchuans didn't just accept me; they embraced me wholeheartedly. Their acceptance wasn't something conditional or measured --- it was freely given, a reflection of the love they carried for one another and those they brought into their lives. In their presence, I felt an unspoken understanding, a reassurance that I belonged.

Love was at the center of everything they did. It was in the way they cared for each other, in the way they listened without judgment, and in the way they uplifted those around them. Their love was expressed in words and actions- always generous, always genuine. Through them, I learned that love isn't just about grand gestures but about showing up, being present, and making others feel valued.

Nurturing And Intelligence: The Gifts Of Wisdom

The Unchuans were natural nurturers. Whether through their kindness, encouragement, or ability to make a house feel like a home, they had a way of making everyone feel supported. They taught me true strength lies in compassion; nurturing those around you is one of your greatest gifts.

At the same time, they carried an undeniable intelligence that extended beyond academics and into how they lived their lives. They thoughtfully approached challenges, made wise decisions, and encouraged intellectual curiosity. Their intelligence wasn't just about knowledge; it was about understanding people and the world and navigating both gracefully.

Professionalism And Fairness: Integrity In Action

One of the greatest lessons I learned from the Unchuans was the value of professionalism and fairness. They carried themselves with integrity, always striving to do what was right, not just what was convenient. Whether in their careers or personal interactions, they treated others with respect and fairness, setting an example of how success is measured by achievements and how one conducts themselves.

They believed in giving people the benefit of the doubt, listening before judging, and standing firm on principles that mattered. Through them, I learned that fairness isn't about treating everyone the same --- it's about recognizing individual needs, showing empathy, and ensuring that kindness and justice go hand in hand.

The Joy Of Fun: A Life Well-Lived

While the Unchuans taught me the importance of values like love, wisdom, and fairness, they also taught me something just as valuable --- the importance of fun. Life, to them, was not just about responsibilities and obligations but laughter, adventure, and shared joy.

Whether through family gatherings, celebrations, or the simple pleasure of being together, they knew how to make every moment meaningful. Their ability to balance work and play, seriousness and lightheartedness, made life with them enriching and deeply enjoyable.

A Lasting Gratitude

Looking back, I am grateful for the Unchuans and the values they passed on to me. They didn't just welcome me into their family— they enriched my life with their wisdom, love, and unwavering support. Their example has shaped the way I view relationships, the way I navigate challenges, and the way I strive to be a better person every day.

To be part of their family is a blessing I will never take for granted. The values they live by are now a part of me, and I will always be grateful for that.

A Friendship Worth More Than Gold

When I first met Frank DiSanto, I wasn't attracted to him. I kept my distance. He was elite in his profession --- sharp, respected, the kind of executive who commanded a room with quiet confidence. And me? I struggled with low self-esteem, constantly questioning whether I belonged in the same space as men like him. Something was intimidating about his presence, and I assumed we had little in common beyond the workplace.

But Life Has A Way Of Surprising You.

Over time, I started to notice things about Frank that I hadn't allowed myself to see before. Beneath his professional polish was a man of immense generosity --- not just with material things, but with his time, wisdom, and support. He didn't just lead; he lifted others. And before I knew it, he was lifting me as well.

Frank became more than a colleague. He became a mentor, guiding me through leadership challenges and helping me build the confidence I lacked. Frank saw potential in me that I hadn't yet seen in myself. Instead of letting me flounder in self-doubt, he pushed me forward, teaching me how to navigate the complexities of being an executive.

But our friendship wasn't just about work. It was about laughter, competition, and the simple joy of shared experiences. We bowled together (he was terrific), played golf, and spent countless evenings on the softball field, reveling in the thrill of the game and the easy camaraderie between us. Whether we were cracking jokes, swapping stories, or just enjoying each other's company, there was an authenticity to our friendship that was rare and invaluable.

Some friendships are built on convenience. Others on shared interests. But the best ones --- the ones that truly matter --- are built on trust, respect, and an unspoken understanding that you're better because of each other. That's the kind of friendship Frank and I shared.

Looking back, I'm grateful that life placed him in my path. I may not have seen it initially, but Frank DiSanto wasn't just a great executive --- he was the best friend I could have asked for. And in the end, that meant more than any title ever could.

5

Individual barriers to gratitude

"We can complain because rose bushes have thorns or rejoice because thorns have roses."
— **Alphonse Karr**, but often attributed to **Abraham Lincoln**.

"Feeling gratitude and not expressing it is like wrapping a present and not giving it."
—William Arthur Ward.

"Gratitude is the healthiest of all human emotions. The more you express gratitude for what you have, the more likely you will have even more to express gratitude for."
—Zig Ziglar

"Gratitude and fear cannot exist in the same space. When you are grateful, fear disappears, and abundance appears."
—Tony Robbins.

"Gratitude is the antidote to fear."
—Melody Beattie.

Gratitude is often spoken of as a simple, natural act that flows effortlessly from a heart full of appreciation. However, for many, expressing gratitude is not as easy as it seems. There are various barriers, both internal and external, that can prevent a person from acknowledging and articulating their thankfulness. Understanding these obstacles is crucial for anyone who wishes to cultivate a life enriched by gratitude.

1. Pride And Ego

One of the most common barriers to expressing gratitude is pride. Some individuals find it challenging to acknowledge the contributions of others because they feel it diminishes their accomplishments. Accepting help or recognizing the impact of someone else's generosity can feel like an admission of weakness or dependence, challenging the notion of self-sufficiency.

The negative impact of pride and ego can be significant. People too proud to express gratitude may struggle to build meaningful relationships, as others may perceive them as ungrateful or arrogant. This practice can lead to isolation, as people are less likely to extend kindness to someone who never acknowledges it. Additionally, pride can stunt personal growth, preventing individuals from recognizing their limitations and learning from others. Without humility, people may find themselves stuck in a cycle of self-importance that limits their ability to connect with and appreciate those around them. Over time, this can create an emotional distance that makes it even harder to foster a genuine sense of gratitude.

2. Fear Of Vulnerability

Expressing gratitude requires openness and sincerity, which some people find uncomfortable. Gratitude is deeply personal and revealing and can make a person feel exposed. The fear of being perceived as overly emotional, sentimental, or weak can prevent someone from sharing their appreciation. This fear is especially true in cultures or environments emphasizing stoicism and independence.

This fear can have a profound negative impact on a person's well-being. Individuals who avoid vulnerability may struggle to form deep and meaningful relationships. Suppressing emotions, including gratitude, can lead to feelings of isolation and emotional disconnect. Over time, this can contribute to stress, anxiety, and even resentment as unexpressed emotions build up. Additionally, those who withhold gratitude may miss out on the positive reinforcement and joy that comes from strengthening bonds with others.

3. A Sense Of Entitlement

Some individuals struggle with gratitude because they have an ingrained sense of entitlement. When people believe they are owed something --- whether it be kindness, support, or opportunities--- they may not feel the need to express appreciation. They see the good they receive as a given rather than a gift, making gratitude seem unnecessary or irrelevant.

This mindset can have several negative consequences. A sense of entitlement can breed dissatisfaction, as individuals focus more on what they believe they lack than what they have. It can lead to strained relationships, as others may feel unappreciated or taken for granted. Furthermore, entitlement can stifle personal growth by preventing individuals from recognizing the value of effort, humility, and reciprocity. Without gratitude, they may miss opportunities to form deeper connections and experience the fulfillment that comes from acknowledging the kindness of others.

4. Busyness And Distraction

Modern life is filled with distractions and demands that can make gratitude an afterthought. People are often too consumed with their responsibilities, challenges, and personal ambitions to pause and acknowledge the kindnesses extended to them. In the rush of daily life, gratitude can be unintentionally overlooked.

A person who is overly busy and distracted misses out on the more profound experiences of life. They may fail to recognize the beauty of small moments, the kindness of others, and the simple joys that bring meaning to everyday life. By constantly rushing, they forgo opportunities to connect with loved ones, reflect on their blessings, and fully engage in the present moment. Over time, this can lead to emptiness or dissatisfaction, as they may accomplish tasks but struggle to find fulfillment in them. Additionally, relationships may suffer when expressions of gratitude are neglected, leaving others feeling unappreciated or unnoticed.

5. Negative Mindset Or Resentment

Gratitude is difficult to express when a person is consumed by resentment, bitterness, or negativity. If someone feels wronged by life, they may struggle to recognize the good that exists around them. Focusing on what is lacking rather than what they have can create a mental block against gratitude.

The negative impact of a persistent negative mindset and resentment is far-reaching. When people harbor bitterness, they may isolate themselves from positive experiences and people, seeing the world through a lens of dissatisfaction. This perspective often leads to chronic stress, anxiety, and even depression, as resentment feeds into a cycle of negativity. Additionally, relationships can suffer because resentment creates emotional walls that prevent meaningful connections. Others may feel the weight of a person's negativity and withdraw, further reinforcing feelings of loneliness and discontent. Over time, this mindset erodes a person's ability to find joy, appreciate the good in their lives, and recognize acts of kindness, ultimately depriving them of the many benefits gratitude can bring.

6. Lack Of Awareness Or Reflection

Gratitude requires mindfulness. Some people do not express appreciation simply because they do not take the time to reflect on what others have done for them. Gratitude can remain dormant without consciously acknowledging the good in one's life.

A lack of awareness or reflection diminishes a person's desire to live a life full of gratitude. It keeps them focused on what is missing rather than what is present. When individuals fail to take stock of the kindness they receive, the blessings in their lives, or the joy they experience, they are less likely to feel appreciative. Over time, this can create a sense of emptiness, as life's richness is overlooked in favor of constant striving or dissatisfaction. Reflection is a powerful tool for cultivating gratitude, as it allows individuals to recognize the efforts of others, appreciate their journey, and develop a sense of contentment. Without this practice, gratitude remains an afterthought rather than a guiding principle for a fulfilling life.

7. Cultural And Familial Influences

In some cultures or family structures, gratitude is not openly expressed. Suppose a person grows up in an environment where appreciation is rarely verbalized or shown. In that case, they may not develop the habit of expressing it. Instead, they may assume that gratitude is understood rather than needing to be explicitly stated. In certain cultures, expressions of gratitude may even be considered unnecessary, with appreciation implied through actions rather than words. While this may work within those contexts, it can create difficulties when interacting with individuals from different backgrounds who expect overt acknowledgments of kindness.

Familial influences also play a significant role. A child raised in a household where gratitude is not modeled or encouraged may grow up without seeing its value. Conversely, if appreciation is only expressed in certain situations --- such as after receiving material gifts --- an individual may struggle to recognize the need to show appreciation for intangible acts of kindness, such as emotional support or mentorship. Over time, these ingrained habits can make it difficult for someone to break free from their early conditioning and develop a more expansive sense of gratitude.

8. Fear Of Rejection Or Misinterpretation

Sometimes, people hesitate to express gratitude because they worry about how it will be received. Will their words be seen as excessive or insincere? Will the recipient feel awkward or dismissive? These doubts can prevent someone from sharing their appreciation, even when deeply felt.

This fear can create emotional barriers that stifle meaningful connections. When gratitude is withheld due to fear of rejection, both the giver and the recipient lose the opportunity to experience the warmth and affirmation that gratitude fosters. Over time, a person may become hesitant to share their appreciation, leading to missed opportunities for building trust, strengthening relationships, and reinforcing positive interactions. In extreme cases, this reluctance can contribute to a sense of emotional isolation, as the person struggles to acknowledge and celebrate the kindness in their life openly.

Overcoming These Barriers

Recognizing these barriers is the first step to overcoming them. By practicing humility, embracing vulnerability, and making gratitude a conscious habit, individuals can learn to express appreciation more freely. Taking small steps—such as writing a thank-you note, verbalizing appreciation in daily conversations, or reflecting on the positive influences in life—can help build the habit of gratitude.

In conclusion, while gratitude can offer profound emotional and psychological benefits, numerous barriers can hinder its consistent cultivation. These obstacles may stem from personal struggles such as negative thought patterns, past traumas, or a lack of self-awareness. External factors, including societal pressures, cultural norms, or a fast-paced, achievement-driven environment, can also discourage individuals from focusing on what they have rather than what they lack. Overcoming these barriers requires intentional effort, mindfulness, and sometimes a shift in perspective. Yet, with persistence, individuals can navigate these challenges and unlock the transformative power of gratitude, leading to enhanced well-being and deeper connections with themselves and others.

As discussed in this chapter, my life has been filled with numerous obstacles to gratitude. I will share two significant periods that are strong examples of this struggle. These moments act as bookends to the story of my life's journey.

A Child Who Struggled To Find Himself

From the beginning, my life was shaped by obstacles that made it difficult to find gratitude. My earliest years were marked by struggle, beginning with the absence of my biological father. Though I was too young to understand his absence, I felt the void he left behind. My world felt incomplete without him, and I often questioned what it would have been like to grow up with his presence and guidance.

As if that loss weren't enough, my health became another hurdle. During my first year of life, I suffered from asthma, a condition that made every breath a challenge. My mother, a determined and loving woman, made the painful decision to leave our small-town home in Virginia and move to New York City. She did so to earn enough money to provide for me, but it came at a cost—we would no longer live together. From then on, I only saw her on certain holidays and a few weeks in the summer.

Growing up without my mother's daily presence left me feeling abandoned, even though I knew she was making sacrifices for my well-being. I longed for her hugs, her laughter, and her reassurance. The separation planted a seed of low self-esteem that would follow me for years. I often felt unworthy of love and attention, questioning if I wasn't enough for my mother to stay.

School only deepened my struggles. I was the smallest boy in my class, often overshadowed by my peers, both physically and socially. To make things worse, I was also one of the youngest, making me feel even more out of place. I watched as others excelled effortlessly during these school years while I battled my insecurities. The combination of my size, my self-doubt, and my yearning for acceptance made each school day feel like an uphill battle.

Whenever things went wrong, my immediate reaction was anger. I felt as though life had singled me out, throwing obstacles my way while others seemed to move forward efficiently. My frustration turned into bitterness, and instead of seeking solutions, I lashed out or withdrew. However, my greatest fear was not my anger—it was failure. I was terrified of falling short—of confirming the negative thoughts I had about myself. The fear of failure became a constant weight, preventing me from taking risks or fully embracing opportunities.

With so many barriers in my way, gratitude felt like a distant concept reserved for those whose lives were free of struggle. I couldn't see beyond my hardships, failing to recognize the strength I was developing. It would take years for me to understand that gratitude was still possible, even in the face of adversity. Still, at that time, it felt like an unreachable destination.

Cancer: My Senior Roadblock To Gratitude

As I matured, gratitude came more easily. I had built a career, nurtured a family, and cherished the love and wisdom of those who shaped me. I had learned to appreciate the trials as much as the triumphs, believing that even hardships carried lessons.

But then came the diagnosis.

March of my 76th year brought news that no one wants to hear --- prostate cancer. At first, I met it with resolve. Surgery in July felt like a step toward victory, a way to solve the problem and move forward. I had always been practical, a man who handled what needed handling. So, I focused on recovery and moving past this chapter.

But cancer had other plans.

On the first day of my 77th year, I learned that a few cancer cells remained. The fight wasn't over. Instead of relief, I found myself plunged into a new battle, one I hadn't expected. The day after Thanksgiving, I started hormone treatment, a two-year sentence to a body and mind not entirely his own. July --- the anniversary of my prostate removal --- would bring radiation. A whole year later, the finish line still seemed far away.

Gratitude became difficult.

Fear crept in first --- fear of what might come and the unknown. Sadness followed, weighing heavily on my chest making me question why this was happening to me. Stress took root, stealing my sleep and gnawing at my peace. Worry made itself a constant companion. And then came the most insidious thought of all: *Why me?*

I had spent my life finding blessings at every turn. But this? This experience was different. It was easy to be grateful when life was good, but how could I be thankful when each day felt like a battle?

And yet, even in the most challenging moments, something within me resisted complete despair. The hands of those who loved me still reached for me. The values I had lived by --- resilience, faith, perseverance --- still guided me. I slowly began to see gratitude wasn't about pretending everything was fine. It was about finding light in the darkness, even when it flickered dimly.

The journey wasn't over, and the road remained uncertain. But as I faced each step, I realized that gratitude wasn't gone even amid fear, sadness, stress, and worry. It was just waiting for me to find it again.

6

THREE GOOD THINGS

"Enjoy the little things, for one day you may look back and realize they were the big things."
—Robert Brault.

"Happiness is not something ready-made. It comes from your own actions."
—Dalai Lama.

"The more you practice the art of thankfulness, the more you have to be thankful for."
—Norman Vincent Peale.

"Reflect upon your present blessings, of which every man has plenty; not on your past misfortunes, of which all men have some."
—Charles Dickens.

Gratitude is a powerful emotion, capable of transforming perspectives and shifting focus from what is lacking to what is abundant. Among the many techniques for cultivating gratitude, one of the most effective and accessible is the practice known as "Three Good Things." This simple yet profound exercise involves reflecting on and documenting three positive events or moments at the end of each day. It may seem straightforward, but its impact on mental and emotional well-being is significant.

The Science Behind "Three Good Things"

Positive psychology research has extensively explored the benefits of gratitude practices, with "Three Good Things" standing out as particularly potent. Studies have shown that consistently engaging in this exercise can improve mood, enhance sleep, increase resilience, and even reduce symptoms of anxiety and depression. The reason behind these benefits lies in the way the brain processes information.

Human beings have a natural negativity bias --- a tendency to focus more on negative experiences than positive ones. This bias is an evolutionary safeguard, ensuring that potential dangers are prioritized. However, modern life often leads to excessive worry, stress, and a skewed perception of reality. The "Three Good Things" practice helps counteract this bias by training the brain to notice and appreciate positive experiences, thereby rewiring neural pathways towards greater optimism and contentment.

How "Three Good Things" Enhances Gratitude

Gratitude is more than just saying "thank you." It is an intentional shift in focus, a conscious recognition of the good in life. The "Three Good Things" practice enhances gratitude in several key ways:

1. Encourages Reflection – Identifying three positive things each day requires introspection. This practice cultivates awareness of the big or small blessings that might go unnoticed. Whether it is a kind word from a friend, a successful task at work, or the sun's warmth on one's face, the practice encourages a deeper appreciation for life's simple joys.
2. Builds a Gratitude Habit – Like any skill, gratitude strengthens with practice. By making "Three Good Things" a daily ritual, gratitude becomes an ingrained habit rather than an occasional sentiment. Over time, this repeated practice helps reshape one's overall outlook, making gratitude a default mindset.
3. Fosters Positivity in Challenging Times – Life is not without difficulties, but gratitude can serve as a buffer against adversity. On tough days, when stress and hardship

dominate, the practice of identifying three good things forces a shift in perspective. Even in the darkest times, there are often moments of kindness, beauty, or progress to acknowledge, however small.

4. Encourages Mindfulness – Practicing gratitude through "Three Good Things" aligns closely with mindfulness. One develops a greater sense of presence and fulfillment by paying attention to the present moment and appreciating positive experiences as they unfold. This practice helps individuals move beyond autopilot living, where days blur together without consciously acknowledging their worth.

Practical Steps To Implement "Three Good Things"

While the practice is simple, consistency is key. Here are some steps to effectively integrate "Three Good Things" into daily life:

1. Choose a Time – The best time to reflect on three good things is typically at the end of the day, allowing for a full review of joyous moments. Many people incorporate it into their nighttime routine, perhaps in a journal or simply in quiet contemplation before sleep.
2. Write It Down – While mentally noting three good things is beneficial, writing them down enhances the impact. A gratitude journal allows for deeper reflection and serves as a tangible record of positivity to revisit during difficult times.
3. Be Specific – The more detailed the reflection, the more meaningful it becomes. Instead of writing "I'm grateful for my friend," specifying "I'm grateful for the unexpected call from my friend today that made me laugh and feel supported" deepens the sense of appreciation.
4. Acknowledge Different Types of Good Things – They need not always be grand or life-changing. A good thing could be as simple as a delicious meal, a moment of peace, or an

achievement, however small. This variety helps maintain engagement with the practice.

5. Make It a Shared Activity – Sharing "Three Good Things" with a partner, family member, or friend can enhance its effects. It fosters connection and encourages a collective focus on gratitude, reinforcing relationship positivity.

The Long-Term Benefits Of "Three Good Things"

Incorporating "Three Good Things" into daily life has immediate and long-term effects. Over time, individuals who practice this consistently report increased life satisfaction, improved relationships, and a stronger sense of well-being. It shifts the mental framework from scarcity to abundance, complaints to appreciation, and stress to contentment.

By consciously recognizing and celebrating daily moments of goodness, gratitude becomes more than just a fleeting emotion- it becomes a way of life. The "Three Good Things" practice, though simple in execution, can reshape perspectives, foster resilience, and bring forth a more grateful and joyful existence.

I want to introduce an article titled *"Try Identifying Three Good Things Each Evening to Boost Happiness,"* published on July 10, 2024, by Katie Kerwin McCrimmon of UCHealth. I believe this piece beautifully conveys the positive impact of the Three Good Things practice. Take a look for yourself!

Is it possible to become a more positive, hopeful person?

Yes. Research shows that by deliberately focusing on good things in your life, you can become happier.

Embracing optimism and your role in making the world a better place is a valuable tool.

A simple tool called 'Three Good Things.'

Dr. Annie Moore helps her patients boost their positive attitudes and resiliency while reducing harmful self-criticism through a daily exercise called "Three Good Things."

It's a simple exercise that can take just a couple of minutes each evening before bed. Highlighting Three Good Things each day can yield long-lasting health benefits.

Moore is an internal medicine doctor at CU Denver Internal Medicine Group near Denver's Cherry Creek neighborhood. She is also a Professor of Clinical Practice at the University of Colorado School of Medicine and did a fellowship in integrative medicine at the University of Arizona. Integrative medicine doctors are trained to focus on the whole person and partner with patients to help them adopt lifestyle changes that can make them healthier.

"We look at root causes for health problems, in addition to giving patients a diagnosis and treatment plan. We hope to understand why a patient gets an illness, especially a chronic illness, in the first place," Moore said.

Researchers in positive psychology tested 'Three Good Things,' and it worked.

Moore first learned about the Three Good Things tool when she worked at Duke University Medical Center. Experts there encourage healthcare workers to use Three Good Things to prevent burnout.

Happiness researcher Dr. Martin Seligman pioneered and tested the Three Good Things tool. He and his team at the University of Pennsylvania Positive Psychology Center did randomized controlled trials to measure the effectiveness of simple interventions that might make people happier. They published their findings in 2005 in American Psychologist.

In their experiment, the researchers randomly assigned participants to try one of six interventions, including a control group that simply wrote in journals about their childhood. One group did the Three Good Things exercise each evening for one week. Then, researchers measured how all the study participants did over time. One month after the study subjects wrote down their Three Good Things each evening for a week, participants "were happier and less depressed than they had been at baseline, and they stayed happier and less depressed at the three-month and six-month follow-ups," the researchers found.

Harsh self-criticism harms health.

Moore started using Three Good Things at Duke and brought the practice with her when she came to Colorado in 2015. In addition to benefiting personally, she likes using Three Good Things with patients who are especially hard on themselves.

"Commonly, we hear a loud inner critic among our patients," Moore said. "Through what they say, they imply, 'I'm not good enough. I'm not meeting my expectations.'"

And, says Moore, that negativity "impedes progress" toward improving health.

"The more you feel like a failure, the more you're going to fail. The goal of Three Good Things is to build back confidence and increase motivation to help people feel more empowered to take positive actions in their lives," Moore said.

How does Three Good Things work?

So, how exactly does a person use the Three Good Things tool?

The concept is easy, and individuals can personalize how they use Three Good Things. The researchers who first tested Three Good Things required study participants to write down three things each evening. By doing the exercise toward the end of the day and before bed, they felt participants would sleep better.

Moore doesn't always write hers down, but when she has in the past, she has enjoyed going back to reading previous lists.

Also, to count a deed as one of your Three Good Things, you must embrace your role as the director of your life.

"The core aspect of this is that it's something we made happen or were actively involved in," Moore said.

So, if the sunrise was beautiful, you can enjoy that but can't list that as one of your Three Good Things since you didn't play a role in bringing on a new day or turning the sky pink and orange.

Not a gratitude journal; Three Good Things requires intention and action

Moore said some people misunderstand Three Good Things as a gratitude journal or a way to appreciate blessings. Certainly, it's great to be thankful, but Three Good Things is different.

"This requires more intention," Moore said.

To be effective, you must recall actions such as carving out time for exercise, calling a friend, picking up groceries for a neighbor, or skipping an unhealthy habit like smoking a cigarette.

"The role we have in creating positive choices is a critical aspect of this," Moore said. "The empowerment and resiliency benefits come from recognizing our role in how we think and act."

Some people only do the exercise for one week, and that's OK. But for others, it becomes a cherished daily practice.

"We see positive outcomes," Moore said. "The idea is that once you notice the positive things you do, you'll choose to do more, and you will see more positive things others do as well. This requires action on a person's part to see the positive, which is critical to resilience."

What if I'm feeling hopeless?

For anyone who feels they have severe depression, call your doctor or seek immediate help elsewhere. Anyone who is having suicidal thoughts can get help 24/7 through the National Suicide Prevention Lifeline at 800-273-8255.

For most people, it's normal to feel somewhat depressed during major life events, natural disasters, and pandemics. Using Three Good Things won't erase sorrows, Moore said. Rather, it's a practice that can help people cope better.

"We can say, 'This is terrible and tragic.' And, at the same time, at the end of each day, we can also say, 'There were Three Good Things in which I participated to make my work and the world better.'"

Who can benefit from Three Good Things?

Everyone.

Moore sees some patients who are coping with complex genetic health challenges. They sometimes feel hopeless.

"They might say, 'I have high cholesterol. No matter what, I'm going to have a heart attack and diabetes. I'm going to die young.'"

Moore tells them that while acknowledging they inherited a tough genetic deck of hands, they can also improve their health and lives.

"They can feel more empowered to minimize the genetic impact, understanding that most health outcomes are lifestyle-based. A lot of people are defeatist these days. There is a balance between owning health challenges and maximizing our health choices to live the best life we can," Moore said.

She also sees patients who have avoided going to a doctor for years because they are embarrassed about their weight or they are dealing with addictions to alcohol or drugs.

An older patient might also be struggling with balance. A patient of any age who has had a challenging surgery might be depressed about a difficult recovery.

For people in these circumstances, one good thing to celebrate can be as simple as getting out of bed.

And we can all do good things to fight social isolation.

"You can write a note to a friend or arrange an outdoor lunch. Taking the initiative to have some social contact is great," Moore said. "The list of ideas for good things is endless."

The concept of positive psychology doesn't mean that you will go around feeling positive all the time.

"Some people find they are living in one ongoing negative emotional state. It can be great to balance the sadness with positive thinking," Moore said.

How long do you have to do Three Good Things?

In the original clinical trial, study volunteers did the Three Good Things for seven consecutive nights. Some continued voluntarily. Even if the participants stopped after a week, the benefits continued. Noticing good things seems to stick with us and improve our attitudes over the long term.

Do you have to do Three Good Things every day?

Yes. To do the activity correctly, you are supposed to do it every day for at least 7 days in a row.

Can you pick the same Three Good Things every day?

No. You need to pick new good things each day.

Do you have to do Three Good Things before bed?

Most advocates for Three Good Things say it's best to do the exercise before bed. Focusing on good things clears your head and drives stress away, thus helping people sleep better. But Moore isn't a purist. If a patient is a morning person and will be more dedicated to focusing on Three Good Things in the morning, then that can work too, she said.

What kind of results have doctors seen?

Seligman's clinical trial showed that doing Three Good Things resulted in greater happiness as measured six months later. Some medical experts say Three Good Things can be as effective as anti-depressants.

Moore has seen excellent results among her patients, whether they have naturally sunny dispositions or tend to see the world pessimistically.

"Everyone can see the world more positively. Hope and confidence overlap," Moore said.

"You can do this on your own. You can do it with your family. It's not going to make bad things go away. But, it does help you cope better with them."

This story was first published on Sept. 11, 2020.

I want to present *Three Good Things* by first expressing my gratitude for three experiences that have significantly impacted my life differently. After that, I will share my appreciation for events today, March 7, 2025.

A Silent Gift

My father was a shadow—an absence rather than a presence for much of my life. My mother divorced him when I was just a few months old, and that was the last time he was ever part of my story. I never met him, heard his voice, or knew the shape of his hands or the weight of his embrace. What I did know was the void he left behind.

As a child, I didn't have a name for what I felt, only that something was missing. I watched other boys toss a baseball with their fathers, heard stories of dad-and-son fishing trips, and saw how my friends' fathers beamed with pride at their accomplishments. I convinced myself I didn't need what they had. But deep inside, I felt the weight of something unspoken --- a longing, a question without an answer.

That void shaped me in ways I wouldn't fully understand until much later. It chipped away at my confidence and made me question my worth. Without a father to guide me, I stumbled through mistakes, searching for validation in places that could never fill the emptiness. I made choices driven by insecurity, by the silent echoes of a father who was never there to tell me I was enough.

However, time and life reveal the truth in unexpected ways. With maturity came reflection, and with reflection came gratitude. The absence that once felt like a curse became a lesson, a teacher in its own right. It forced me to seek strength within myself, forge my path, and learn resilience in ways I might not have otherwise.

Most of all, it allowed me to recognize and address my struggles with self-worth. Had my father been present, perhaps I wouldn't have been forced to confront those parts of myself. But because he wasn't, I had to learn --- through trial, failure, and introspection. And in learning, I grew.

Today, I can say something I never thought I would: *Thank you.* Thank you for giving me life. Thank you for the struggles because they led to wisdom. Thank you for the mistakes; they became my most excellent teachers. Your absence was painful, but it was also instructive. And in the end, it helped shape the person I have become.

Sometimes, the most profound gifts come from what we never had.

Mary's Memory

Mary was more than just a childhood friend—she was a part of my story, woven into the fabric of my earliest memories. She was the niece of Uncle Jack's sports buddy. Still, she was the girl who could outrun me in a race, make me laugh until my stomach hurt, and turn the most ordinary afternoons into adventures. We played together endlessly, running through the neighborhood, inventing games, and sharing the pure, unfiltered joy that only childhood can bring.

As we grew older, our friendship deepened. Early in our teenage years, we stepped into something new --- we went on our first dates together. It was awkward, exciting, and unforgettable. Mary would forever be the girl I shared that milestone with, making it a memory I would cherish forever.

Not long after, we were invited to go to the skating rink with some of our friends. It was supposed to be another night of fun, laughter, and youthful excitement. I wanted to go --- of course I did. But my grandmother, with the firm yet loving wisdom that only grandmothers possess, said no. I was disappointed, frustrated even. I didn't understand why she wouldn't let me go.

That night, everything changed. On the drive home from the skating rink, their car was involved in a tragic accident. There was only one survivor. Mary was gone.

Grief and sadness consumed me. The weight of it was unbearable. How could someone so full of life, so important to me, be taken away instantly? The unfairness of it all was too much to comprehend.

Yet, with time, I found a way to hold onto something beyond the pain. As devastating as the loss was, it allowed me to appreciate what Mary had given me in her short time on this earth. I focused on the laughter, the games, and the excitement of our first dates --- moments that will be ever-present in my mind. No matter what, she would always be a part of my story. She would always be my first date.

I also grew to understand the depth of my grandmother's love. What once felt like an unfair restriction became an undeniable blessing. She protected me in a way I couldn't see then, and I am endlessly grateful.

Most of all, I found peace knowing that Mary had found hers. I do not doubt that she rests in the arms of God, in a place of eternal light and love. Though she was taken too soon, she is not lost --- she is simply beyond my reach for now. And until the day we meet again, I will carry her memory with me, forever grateful for the time we shared.

Herbert: A Man Of Wisdom And Devotion

I was sixteen when my mother remarried. The decision wasn't hers alone --- she had my full approval. Herbert was a quiet but commanding presence, with intelligence evident in everything he did. He was a member of Mensa, and his mind constantly explored ideas that few could follow. Yet, for all his intellect, his greatest gift was the love Herbert gave my mother. That love never wavered, not for a moment, until the day he passed at the age of 92.

Herbert's mind was both a blessing and a curse. He had the capacity for extraordinary business success. Still, his thoughts often pulled him in another direction --- a world of protectionism, of shielding what he valued most. It was as if he saw threats where others saw an opportunity, unable to fully commit to the paths that might have led to greater prosperity. Even so, his wisdom was undeniable, and I, in my emerging adult years, was fortunate to learn from him.

What I didn't know was that he was a war hero. He had fought in World War II --- a young soldier in a brutal conflict, but he never once spoke of his role. It wasn't until later in his life that my mother revealed the truth: Herbert had been awarded the Silver Star for bravery in Germany. He had risked his life in ways I could scarcely imagine, yet he carried no airs of self-importance. Herbert never sought recognition. In his mind, he had done what was right.

Herbert's humility, intellect, and unwavering love for my mother shaped me in ways I didn't fully understand until later in life. He was more than a stepfather; he was a mentor, a guide, and an example of quiet strength. I will always be grateful for the wisdom he shared, the values he instilled, and the steadfast presence he provided in my life.

Even now, I think of him often, knowing that his influence will never fade.

Three Good Things I Am Grateful For Today – March 7, 2025

1. **A Healthy Start to the Day**
   I woke up feeling happy and healthy, and my blood sugar was under control. Each morning that begins this way is a gift; I don't take it for granted. It sets the tone for the rest of the day, allowing me to focus on what truly matters.

2. **My Wife's Survival and Strength**
   Today, I am overwhelmingly grateful that my wife is recovering from a pacemaker operation that occurred three days after she had a heart valve replacement. By the grace of God, she is on the road to recovery. Her resilience and the quick actions of her medical team were nothing short of a miracle.

3. **Family Bonding in the Face of Adversity**
   During my wife's recovery, our core family came together in a way that deepened our bond. The love, support, and presence of those closest to us provided comfort and strength during a challenging time. These moments remind me of the power of family and the unbreakable connections that sustain us.

Today, I am reminded that life is precious, love is enduring, and each new day is a blessing.

7

UNDERSTAND YOURSELF GRATEFULLY

"Gratitude turns what we have into enough."
—Aesop.

"When I started counting my blessings, my whole life turned around."
—Willie Nelson.

"The more you praise and celebrate your life, the more there is in life to celebrate."
—Oprah Winfrey.

"The roots of all goodness lie in the soil of appreciation for goodness."
—Dalai Lama.

Understanding oneself is a lifelong journey, but doing so with gratitude transforms that journey into something profound and fulfilling. When we approach self-discovery with appreciation, we cultivate self-awareness, resilience, contentment, and a deeper connection with the world around us. Gratitude allows us to see our strengths and weaknesses with kindness, fostering personal growth without harsh self-judgment.

At the heart of this process lies *self-reflection* --- the conscious act of examining our thoughts, emotions, and actions to gain insight into who we are. Self-reflection and gratitude provide clarity, balance, and a more purposeful approach to life.

The Role Of Gratitude In Self-Understanding

Gratitude shifts our perspective from focusing on what we lack to appreciating what we have. In the context of self-reflection, this means acknowledging our good and bad experiences as valuable lessons that contribute to our growth. When we examine ourselves with gratitude, we develop self-compassion and a willingness to embrace change.

Consider the difference between these two perspectives:

1. Self-Reflection Without Gratitude: "I failed at my goal. I always make mistakes and don't know why I even try."
2. Self-Reflection With Gratitude: "I didn't achieve my goal this time but learned what doesn't work. This experience is an opportunity to improve, and I'm grateful for the lesson."

By choosing gratitude, we transform our setbacks into opportunities rather than stumbling blocks.

Life is full of setbacks—failed attempts, unexpected challenges, and moments of disappointment. When faced with adversity, it's easy to fall into frustration, self-doubt, or hopelessness. However, gratitude can reframe these difficulties, transforming them from obstacles that hold us back into stepping-stones that propel us forward.

By choosing to approach setbacks with gratitude, we shift our perspective. Instead of viewing failure as a stopping point, we see it as a learning experience, an opportunity for growth, and even a necessary step toward success.

The Importance Of Self-Reflection

Self-reflection is essential for personal growth, emotional well-being, and achieving purpose. It allows us to:

- **Recognize Our Strengths and Weaknesses:** Understanding what we do well and where we struggle helps us navigate life with confidence and humility.
- **Make Better Decisions:** Reflecting on past experiences allows us to learn from them and make wiser choices in the future.

- **Improve Relationships:** When we understand ourselves, we communicate more effectively and foster deeper connections with others.
- **Manage Stress and Emotions:** Reflection helps us process emotions and develop healthier coping mechanisms.
- **Cultivate Inner Peace:** By aligning our actions with our values, we feel more fulfilled and at peace with ourselves.

Without self-reflection, we risk moving through life on autopilot, reacting impulsively rather than responding thoughtfully.

To develop a habit of self-reflection infused with gratitude, consider these strategies:

1. Journaling With Gratitude

Writing down thoughts, experiences, and lessons learned is a powerful reflection method. Each day, ask yourself:

- What went well today?
- What challenges did I face, and what did I learn from them?
- What am I grateful for about myself?

By documenting these reflections, patterns will emerge, helping you understand yourself more deeply.

2. Mindfulness And Meditation

Sitting in stillness and observing your thoughts allows you to process emotions without judgment. Mindful breathing exercises and gratitude meditations can help shift your mindset toward appreciation and self-acceptance.

3. Seeking Feedback From Others

An outside perspective can sometimes provide valuable insights into our behaviors and tendencies. Ask trusted friends, family, or mentors for honest feedback, and receive it with an open heart and gratitude.

4. Celebrating Progress, Not Just Perfection

Recognize that self-growth is a continuous process. Acknowledge how far you've come instead of focusing on what you haven't achieved. Celebrate small wins and appreciate the journey.

5. Practicing Self-Compassion

Being kind to yourself is crucial in self-reflection. Instead of harsh self-criticism, offer yourself the same understanding and encouragement you would give a friend.

Understanding yourself gratefully means embracing all aspects of yourself- your strengths, weaknesses, successes, and failures- with appreciation. Self-reflection, when guided by gratitude, turns life's ups and downs into valuable lessons, fostering personal growth and inner peace.

By regularly looking inward with a grateful heart, you not only deepen your self-awareness but also cultivate a more fulfilling and meaningful life.

The Mindset Shift: From Defeat To Growth

When something doesn't go as planned, our immediate reaction is often frustration or self-criticism. We focus on what went wrong, blaming ourselves or external circumstances. But with gratitude, we can shift that mindset:

- Instead of saying, "I failed; I'm not good enough," gratitude lets us say, "I learned something valuable that will help me improve."
- Instead of saying, "Why did this happen to me?" we can say, "This challenge is shaping me into a stronger, wiser person."

- Instead of dwelling on what we lost, we can focus on what we gained from the experience.

This shift in perspective transforms setbacks into essential parts of our journey rather than insurmountable roadblocks.

How Gratitude Helps Us Reframe Setbacks

1. Finding the Lesson in Every Challenge

Every setback carries a lesson if we are open to seeing it. Gratitude helps us recognize that difficulties teach us resilience, patience, and problem-solving skills. Even when something feels like a failure, there is always an insight we can gain from it.

Example: If you were denied a job after a promising interview, gratitude allows you to see it as an opportunity to improve your skills or seek a position that aligns better with your values and strengths.

2. Strengthening Resilience

Gratitude reminds us that setbacks are temporary and that we have overcome challenges. When we focus on what we still have and what we can learn, we develop the resilience needed to keep moving forward rather than giving up.

Example: An athlete who loses a competition can choose to be grateful for the experience, using it as motivation to train harder and refine their strategy.

3. Keeping Hope Alive

When we practice gratitude, we focus on the bigger picture rather than being consumed by short-term disappointments. This practice prevents setbacks from defining us and keeps us hopeful for the future.

Example: If a business venture doesn't succeed, instead of dwelling on the loss, gratitude helps us appreciate the skills we developed, the connections we made, and the new ideas that emerged, keeping us open to future opportunities.

4. Cultivating Self-Compassion

Many people are their own harshest critics. When we experience setbacks, we often engage in negative self-talk. Gratitude counteracts this by reminding us that our progress, strengths, and setbacks are part of every successful journey.

Example: Instead of thinking, "I always mess things up," gratitude helps us say, "I am doing my best, and I am learning along the way."

5. Encouraging Action Instead of Inaction

Setbacks can paralyze us if we dwell on disappointment. However, gratitude encourages movement. When we are thankful for what we've learned, we are more motivated to take the next step.

Example: A musician who receives criticism on their performance can be grateful for the feedback, using it as inspiration to improve rather than as a reason to quit.

Real-Life Example: Thomas Edison's Perspective On Failure

Thomas Edison, the lightbulb inventor, famously said, "I have not failed. I've just found 10,000 ways that won't work." This mindset embodies the power of gratitude. Instead of viewing failures as defeats, he saw them as necessary steps toward success. Regardless of the outcome, his ability to stay grateful for each experiment enabled him to persist and ultimately achieve greatness.

To conclude, gratitude is more than just an attitude --- it's a tool that transforms how we experience challenges. By choosing to be grateful, we turn setbacks into stepping stones that help us grow, learn, and move forward.

Every difficulty contains a hidden gift. We can uncover those gifts with gratitude, allowing setbacks to shape us into stronger, wiser, and more resilient individuals. Instead of stopping us, setbacks become the very thing that propels us toward success.

The following article, written by Ilene S. Cohen, PhD, captures the essence of the importance of understanding yourself with gratitude. Dr. Cohen . is a psychotherapist and blogger who teaches in the Department of Counseling at Barry University.

The Power Of Self-Reflection

A Personal Perspective: Finding calm amidst the chaos.

In the swirling vortex of turbulence that life can sometimes become, it's easy to get caught up in the whirlwind of emotions, reactions, and rapid-fire decision-making. We often find ourselves casting blame, rushing headlong into solutions, or even avoiding problems outright. However, in those moments of upheaval, it might be time to turn the gaze inward and embark on a journey of self-reflection.

Self-reflection is not just an act of introspection but a voyage back home, deep into the heart of our thoughts, beliefs, and principles. It's when we pause amidst the world's noise, step back, and truly consider our values and the type of person we want to be when things go awry.

Navigating the Storm

When turbulence strikes, it's natural for our worlds to feel shaken. Uncertainty breeds anxiety, and before we know it, we're adrift in a sea of confusion. This is the moment to anchor ourselves on solid ground. It's time to clear away the noise and reflect on our new reality.

Ask yourself, how do you want to respond to this situation? What kind of person do you want to be in the face of adversity? Do you want to be the one marching for your beliefs? Or perhaps the person who remains calm amidst the storm? Maybe you're the listener, the quiet fighter, or the beacon of hope in the face of pain and suffering.

These are not easy questions to answer. They require courage and honesty. But it is through these questions that we begin to understand ourselves better. We start to realize that the best time to express our values is during our most challenging moments because it is then that we show the world who we truly are.

The Power of Reflection

Through self-reflection, we find calm amidst the chaos. It allows us to thoughtfully contemplate underlying issues and devise <u>mindful</u> resolutions. Self-reflection is like a mental sanctuary, engaging our logical minds when emotions threaten to overwhelm us.

Yes, it might be painful at times – looking inward often is. But the clarity it brings is worth the discomfort. It's like cleaning a wound; it might sting initially, but ultimately it promotes healing.

Embrace the Challenge

Today, I challenge you to embark on this journey of self-reflection. Embrace it wholeheartedly. Ask yourself the big questions. Observe your thoughts and feelings without judgment. Listen to what your heart and mind are telling you. Allow yourself to grow from the experience. Decide who you want to be while standing on solid ground.

Remember, self-reflection isn't a one-time event. It's a continuous process, a lifelong journey of understanding ourselves and our place in the world. It's about recognizing our strengths, acknowledging our weaknesses, and striving to become better, stronger, and more <u>resilient</u>.

In the face of turbulence, let's not lose sight of ourselves. Instead, let's turn inward, reflect, and emerge stronger, wiser, and more grounded. After all, true strength lies not in avoiding the storm but in navigating through it with grace, courage, and conviction.

When the world around you seems to be in chaos, remember that the answer may lie within. In the quiet space of self-reflection, you'll find the calm amidst the chaos, the strength to face any challenge, and the <u>wisdom</u> to navigate the turbulent seas of life.

My Self-Reflection Story

It began like any other day. I arrived at the office ready to tackle the financial challenges of a client. My mind was focused, and my routine was uninterrupted. But as the hours passed, an unshakable feeling of confinement crept in. It was like an invisible weight had settled on my chest, pressing down with an unfamiliar urgency. Without understanding why, I decided I needed to leave. Maybe I had an appointment? Perhaps I just needed air? I made my way to my car, but upon reaching it, I realized something unsettling --- I had nowhere to go.

In that moment, an overwhelming sense of loss enveloped me. My direction, purpose, and even my grasp on reality seemed to blur. Defeated, I turned around and walked back into my office. I sat down, and the tears came. I had no control over them, nor did I understand their cause. I only knew that I felt lost.

My administrative assistant, a steady presence in my daily life, found me in this vulnerable state. She didn't ask questions, nor did she offer empty reassurances. Instead, she said something that would alter my course: "I know what you need, but you may not be ready for it." With gentle guidance, she pointed me toward a place I had never expected to go --- a hospital.

As it turned out, this was no ordinary hospital. It was a treatment center for alcohol dependency and psychiatric care. Even as I walked through its doors, I did not yet understand why I was there. It was only after I spoke with a counselor, sharing my history, my struggles, and my fears, that the truth began to emerge. The professionals who assessed me reached a conclusion that was both shocking and undeniable ---I was an alcoholic.

I had always considered myself functional and successful. But their words struck a chord deep within me. Though outwardly stable, my life had been teetering on the edge of peril for longer than I had cared to admit.

It was in this place, among strangers who shared my struggles, that I was introduced to something that would change my life forever --- the Twelve Steps of Alcoholics Anonymous. Though all the steps carried wisdom, it was the first two that resonated most profoundly:

1. We admitted we were powerless over alcohol --- that our lives had become unmanageable.
2. We came to believe that a power greater than ourselves could restore us to sanity.

In those words, I found clarity. They stripped away my excuses, justifications, and tendency to blame others for my misfortunes. They forced me to confront a truth I had long avoided—the problem was within me. But alongside that truth came an incredible realization: I was not alone. There was a power greater than myself that could guide, strengthen, and restore me if I allowed it.

These steps demanded deep self-reflection. They required honesty, humility, and the willingness to change. It was not an easy path, but I discovered something remarkable as I walked- I could heal. With each day, each meeting, and each moment of surrender, I felt the weight lift.

Looking back, I am filled with immense gratitude. Gratitude for the breaking point that led me to seek help. I give gratitude to the assistant who saw what I could not. I am grateful for the program that gave me a framework to rebuild my life. Most of all, I am thankful for the realization that I was never truly alone.

This journey has been one of the greatest gifts I have ever received. It has given me a second chance and a deeper understanding of myself and the grace surrounding me. And for that, I will always be thankful.

8

DELIGHT IN BLESSINGS

"If you're lucky to have three close people in your life, you're blessed."
—Tiger Woods.

"Living in a state of gratitude is the gateway to grace."
—Arianna Huffington.

"There are always flowers for those who want to see them."
— Henri Matisse.

"When we give cheerfully and accept gratefully, everyone is blessed."
— Maya Angelou.

I recently came across a website exploring Biblical Wonders where I found an article entitled: "10 Blessings Found in the 10 Commandments Reflecting Philippians 4:8". It seems to be an appropriate lead into this chapter on the Delight in Blessings. I will now share it with you.

Have you ever wondered how the Ten Commandments can bring blessings into your life?

Did you know these commandments align with the virtues highlighted in Philippians 4:8?

In this article, we will explore the ten blessings that can be found in the Ten Commandments, which guide us toward living a life of integrity, peace, and purity. These commandments foster harmonious relationships and a deep connection with God.

Let's delve into each commandment and discover its blessings, from embracing honesty to cultivating trust, honoring authority figures, upholding justice, fostering purity in relationships, finding contentment, and much more.

Are you ready to uncover the blessings hidden within the Ten Commandments? Let's begin the journey together and explore the profound wisdom contained within these ancient teachings.

Embrace Honesty: "Thou Shalt Not Bear False Witness" (Exodus 20:16)

The commandment "Thou shalt not bear false witness" encourages us to embrace honesty in our words and actions. By doing so, we cultivate trust and integrity in our relationships, building a solid foundation of authenticity and openness.

Honesty forms the bedrock of any healthy relationship, whether it be with family, friends, or colleagues. When we embrace honesty, we commit ourselves to speaking the truth, even when it may be uncomfortable or challenging.

This commitment to truth fosters an environment of openness and transparency, allowing genuine connections to flourish.

When we are honest, we demonstrate our respect for others by providing them with accurate information and sincere feedback.

By being truthful, we avoid causing harm or confusion and promote clarity and understanding. Our words and actions carry weight, and embracing honesty ensures that we wield that influence responsibly.

"Honesty is the first chapter in the book of wisdom." – Thomas Jefferson.

Cultivating trust and integrity through honesty is essential not just in our personal relationships but also in our professional lives. Employers and colleagues value individuals who are trustworthy and reliable. By embracing honesty, we build a reputation for ourselves as people of integrity, furthering our career development and fostering a positive work environment.

Integrity can be defined as the adherence to moral and ethical principles. By embracing honesty, we align our actions with our beliefs and values, creating a sense of internal consistency. This integrity not only strengthens our character but also inspires trust from those around us.

Embracing honesty also contributes to the greater good of society. When collectively cultivating a culture of truth and integrity, we foster a society built on trust and cooperation. This leads to stronger communities and institutions where individuals feel safe and supported.

*Embrace honesty today **and witness the transformative power it has in your relationships, personal growth, and the world around you.***

Honor: "Honour Thy Father And Thy Mother" (Exodus 20:12)

The commandment to honor our parents teaches us the importance of respecting authority figures. Honoring our parents and other authorities contributes to a peaceful and harmonious existence, fostering longevity in our relationships and overall well-being.

Honoring our parents is a sign of gratitude and appreciation for the love and sacrifices they have made for us. It reflects our recognition of their wisdom and guidance, acknowledging their authority in our lives.

Respecting our parents extends beyond mere obedience; it encompasses genuine honor, reverence, and gratitude.

When we honor our parents, we create an environment of mutual respect and understanding, paving the way for healthy and fulfilling relationships. It sets an example for others to follow, demonstrating the importance of respecting authority in all areas of life.

"Respecting authority figures not only brings peace to our lives but also creates a ripple effect of respect and harmony in society."

When we honor those in authority, whether it be our parents, teachers, or leaders, we contribute to the establishment of an orderly and productive community.

Moreover, honoring our parents fosters longevity in our relationships. It strengthens the bond between generations, ensuring that wisdom, values, and traditions are passed down from one generation to the next.

This continuity ensures the preservation of family ties and the enrichment of familial heritage.

Benefits of Honoring Parents	Long-lasting Relationships	Peaceful Existence
1. Strengthened family bonds	Respecting authority promotes peaceful coexistence among family members and society at large.	By honoring our parents, we create an atmosphere of Respect and tranquility
2. Intergenerational wisdom and heritage preservation		
3. Setting a positive example for future generations	Inspiring future generations to respect and honor authority figures, fostering harmony in society.	Children learn the value of peaceful interactions and establish healthy relationships.

Justice: "Thou Shalt Not Steal" (Exodus 20:15)

The commandment "Thou shalt not steal" urges us to uphold justice in our actions. By respecting the property and rights of others, we contribute to a fair and balanced community where everyone is treated with equity and fairness.

The Importance of Justice

Justice is pivotal in creating a harmonious society where everyone's rights are protected and upheld. It embodies the principles of fairness, equality, and accountability, ensuring that no individual is unjustly deprived of what rightfully belongs to them.

In the context of the commandment "Thou shalt not steal," justice calls upon us to recognize and respect the boundaries of personal property. By refraining from taking what is not ours, we create an environment where trust is nurtured, and individuals can thrive without fear of exploitation or loss.

Upholding justice goes beyond avoiding theft; it encompasses the broader concepts of fairness, integrity, and respect. By treating others with dignity and honoring their rights, we contribute to establishing a fair and balanced community.

Building a Fair and Balanced Community

A fair and balanced community is one where justice prevails, fostering an environment of trust, harmony, and cooperation. When we respect the property and rights of others, we lay the foundation for a society that operates on the principles of equity and fairness.

Respecting the boundaries of personal property not only safeguards individuals' possessions but also promotes economic stability and growth. By discouraging theft and encouraging responsible stewardship, we contribute to a thriving economy that benefits all community members.

Furthermore, upholding justice in our actions creates a sense of security and well-being among community members. It allows individuals to live without the constant fear of being victims of theft or injustice, promoting peace and a more contented way of life.

Striving for Justice

Embracing the commandment "Thou shalt not steal" means actively striving for justice in our daily lives. It challenges us to be mindful of the impact our actions have on others and to treat everyone with fairness and respect, regardless of their social status or background.

By instilling a sense of justice in our communities, we foster an inclusive and equitable society where individuals can thrive and flourish. Upholding justice requires us to stand up against injustice, advocate for the rights of the marginalized, and actively work towards building a better and more just world for all.

"Justice is not just an abstract concept; it is a compass that guides us towards creating a fair and balanced community."

A Call to Action

As individuals, we have the power to promote justice in our communities. By upholding the commandment "Thou shalt not steal" and respecting the property and rights of others, we can contribute to establishing a fair and balanced society.

Let us embody justice in our actions, words, and thoughts, promoting fairness, equity, and respect in all aspects of our lives. Together, we can create a world where justice prevails and all individuals can experience the blessings of a fair and balanced community.

Purity: "Thou Shalt Not Commit Adultery" (Exodus 20:14)

The commandment against adultery emphasizes the importance of purity in our relationships. By honoring the commitment and trust within our relationships, we foster deep connections and become trustworthy individuals, cultivating harmonious connections with others.

Deep connections are built on a foundation of trustworthiness and purity. When we commit to being faithful and loyal to our partners, we create an environment of security and love.

Adultery not only violates the sacred bond between two individuals but also erodes the trust and intimacy that are essential in any relationship. By adhering to the commandment "Thou Shalt Not Commit Adultery," we uphold the values of purity and faithfulness, preserving the sanctity of our connections.

Building Trust and Fostering Deep Connections

Trust is the bedrock of any meaningful relationship. When we commit to purity, we demonstrate our trustworthiness and strengthen the bond with our partners:

1. Honest Communication: By fostering open and honest communication, we create a space where both partners can express their needs and concerns, leading to a deeper understanding and connection.
2. Emotional Intimacy: Purity in relationships allows us to be vulnerable with our partners, fostering emotional intimacy and creating a safe space for shared experiences and personal growth.
3. Respecting Boundaries: Respecting boundaries is essential in maintaining trust and preserving the integrity of the relationship. Purity means honoring and valuing our partner's boundaries, ensuring mutual respect and trust.

The Benefits of Purity

Embracing purity in our relationships brings forth numerous benefits that contribute to our overall well-being:

- Increased Emotional Connection: When both partners commit to purity, emotional connections are strengthened, leading to a deeper sense of love and fulfillment.
- Enhanced Intimacy: Purity fosters a healthy and fulfilling physical intimacy, allowing couples to experience a deeper level of closeness and connection.
- Strengthened Trust: By adhering to the commandment against adultery, trust is reinforced, creating a solid foundation for a long-lasting and meaningful relationship.

- *Emotional Security: Purity brings emotional security, as both partners can rely on the faithfulness and commitment of one another, fostering a sense of peace and stability.*

By valuing purity in our relationships, we establish a strong sense of trust, deep connections, and a solid foundation for lasting happiness. Upholding the commandment against adultery not only benefits our relationships but also promotes a society built on trustworthiness and respect.

Loveliness: "Thou Shalt Not Covet" (Exodus 20:17)

The commandment against coveting reminds us of the importance of contentment. By finding joy and peace of mind in what we have, we cultivate a mindset of contentment, bringing loveliness and an inner sense of fulfillment.

"Happiness comes when we stop complaining about the troubles we have and offer thanks for all the troubles we don't have." – Bob Marley.

Embracing the Beauty of Contentment

In a world that often glorifies material possessions and constant striving, the commandment against coveting invites us to pause and appreciate the blessings surrounding us. It reminds us to find contentment in our current circumstances and avoid the pitfall of always wanting more.

- *Counting Your Blessings: Take a moment every day to reflect on what you are grateful for. By shifting your focus to the positives in your life, you can cultivate a sense of contentment and peace.*
- *Practicing Mindfulness: Be present in the moment and fully appreciate what you have. Mindfulness helps you tune in to the richness and loveliness of the present, fostering a more profound sense of fulfillment.*
- *Celebrating Others: Instead of coveting what others have, rejoice in their successes and achievements. Spreading joy and*

acknowledging the accomplishments of others enhances our contentment.

- *Letting Go of Comparison: Each person's journey is unique. Avoid comparing yourself to others and their possessions. Recognize that true fulfillment comes from within, not from external sources.*

By embracing the beauty of contentment, we free ourselves from the constant pursuit of material possessions and find peace in what we already have. Contentment brings loveliness to our lives and allows us to experience true joy and fulfillment.

Benefits of Contentment	Examples in Daily Life
Peace of mind	Happily savoring a home-cooked meal, grateful for nourishment.
Reduced stress and anxiety	Finding delight in simple pleasures like a warm cup of tea or a walk
Stronger relationships	Enjoying quality time with loved ones without distractions or comparison
Increased self-acceptance	Embracing and appreciating your unique qualities and talents

Good Rapport: "Thou Shalt Not Take The Name Of The Lord Thy God In Vain" (Exodus 20:7)

The commandment "Thou Shalt Not Take the Name of the Lord Thy God in Vain" reminds us of the importance of revering God's name. By showing respect and dignity towards God and His name, we cultivate a life filled with reverence and honor, establishing a good rapport among others.

"You shall not take the name of the Lord your God in vain, for the Lord will not hold him guiltless who takes his name in vain." (Exodus 20:7)

Revering God's name goes beyond refraining from using it casually or irreverently. It is about recognizing the divine significance and holiness associated with God's name. When we hold His name in high regard, we demonstrate our deep reverence for His presence and power in our lives.

"The fear of the Lord is the beginning of wisdom; all those who practice it have a good understanding." (Psalm 111:10)

Respecting and honoring God's name also extends to how we speak about Him and the values and beliefs we associate with His name. When we uphold the sanctity of God's name, we contribute to a culture of reverence and honor, fostering a deep sense of spirituality and humility.

Showcasing Reverence and Honor

Revering God's name involves not only refraining from using it carelessly but also living a life that reflects the values and teachings associated with His name. By aligning our thoughts, words, and actions with the principles of love, compassion, justice, and forgiveness, we showcase reverence and honor for God.

In our interactions with others, we can exemplify respect and dignity by treating everyone with kindness, compassion, and fairness. When we honor others as unique creations made in the image of God, we demonstrate the reverence we have for our Creator.

Establishing a Good Rapport

By revering God's name and reflecting His character in our lives, we establish a good rapport among others. Our actions and words testify to our commitment to live in accordance with God's teachings, earning the respect and admiration of those around us.

When we consistently embody reverence and honor in our lives, we become a living testament to the goodness and grace of God. Our relationships reflect God's love, and our interactions become opportunities to share the blessings we have received.

Ultimately, by revering God's name with respect and dignity, we contribute to a world filled with righteousness, love, and peace. Our actions become a testimony to the transforming power of God's presence, leaving a lasting impact on those we encounter.

Virtue: "Thou Shalt Have No Other Gods Before Me" (Exodus 20:3)

The commandment to have no other gods before God is a profound reminder of the importance of loyalty and devotion to Him. By dedicating ourselves wholeheartedly to God and His teachings, we cultivate moral strength and nurture a clear conscience, embodying virtue in our thoughts, words, and actions.

A strong sense of virtue enables us to make choices that align with God's will, allowing us to live a life rooted in righteousness and love. Loyalty to God means placing Him first in our lives, seeking His guidance, and obeying His commandments.

When we prioritize our relationship with God, we develop a deeper understanding of His character and the values He upholds. This understanding empowers us to live a life that reflects His divine virtues, such as love, compassion, forgiveness, and integrity.

Embracing virtue and remaining loyal to God not only brings us closer to Him but also strengthens our connection with others. It allows us to consistently demonstrate kindness, empathy, and humility in our interactions, cultivating harmonious relationships and fostering a sense of unity within our communities.

Moreover, embodying virtue and remaining loyal to God grants us the resilience and moral fortitude needed to navigate the challenges and temptations that life presents. With a clear conscience, we can walk confidently, knowing that our choices align with God's desires for our lives.

Ultimately, by prioritizing virtue and loyalty to God, we strive to become the best versions of ourselves, aligning our lives with His divine plan. Through our steadfast commitment to virtue, we not only experience personal growth and fulfillment but also inspire and uplift others through our words and actions.

Key Takeaways:

- *The commandment to have no other gods before God reminds us of the importance of loyalty and devotion to Him.*
- *By dedicating ourselves to God and His teachings, we cultivate* **moral strength** *and a* **clear conscience***, embodying virtue in our thoughts, words, and actions.*
- *Embracing virtue and remaining loyal to God strengthens our connection with others, fosters harmonious relationships, and promotes unity.*
- *Prioritizing virtue and* **loyalty to God** *grants us the moral fortitude to navigate life's challenges and temptations.*
- *Through steadfast commitment to virtue, we align our lives with God's divine plan, inspiring and uplifting others along the way.*

Praiseworthy: "Remember The Sabbath Day, To Keep It Holy" (Exodus 20:8)

The commandment to remember the Sabbath emphasizes the importance of rest, rejuvenation, and reflection on God's goodness.

By observing the Sabbath, you create precious moments for rest, allowing your mind and body to recharge. It serves as a time for self-care and introspection, enabling you to reflect on your faith, blessings, and purpose in life.

"Remember the Sabbath day, to keep it holy. You shall labor and do all your work in six days, but the seventh day is a Sabbath to the Lord your God. On it you shall not do any work, you, or your son, or your daughter, your male servant, or your female servant, or your livestock, or the sojourner who is within your gates." – Exodus 20:8-10

Observing the Sabbath allows you to disconnect from the busyness of everyday life and find solace in the presence of God. It is a time to appreciate the blessings He has bestowed upon you and express gratitude for His unwavering love and guidance.

By engaging in prayer, studying scripture, and participating in worship, you deepen your spiritual connection and find serenity during life's challenges.

Moreover, the Sabbath serves as a reminder of the sanctity of time. By setting aside this day as holy, you prioritize your relationship with God and acknowledge His sovereignty over all aspects of your life.

The Sabbath is an invitation to surrender control and find solace in the rest that comes from trusting in His divine plan.

Resting on the Sabbath not only benefits your spiritual well-being but also has practical implications for your physical and mental health. It allows you to replenish your energy, reduce stress, and restore balance in your life. Taking time for leisure activities, spending quality time with loved ones, and engaging in activities that bring you joy can contribute to overall well-being and refreshment.

Remember, the Sabbath is not merely a legalistic obligation but a praiseworthy practice that brings harmony and peace. It offers a pause in the busyness of life, allowing you to reflect on your journey, seek God's guidance, and appreciate the blessings surrounding you.

Embracing the Sabbath as a sacred time of rest and rejuvenation enables you to live a life that is praiseworthy in the eyes of God.

Benefits of Observing the Sabbath:

- *Rest and **rejuvenation** for physical and mental well-being*
- *Deepened spiritual connection and **reflection** on God's goodness*
- *Prioritization of your relationship with God*
- *Increased gratitude and appreciation for blessings*
- *Reduced stress and restoration of balance*

- *Quality time spent with loved ones*
- *Opportunity for self-care and leisure activities*

Righteousness: "Thou Shalt Not Kill" (Exodus 20:13)

The commandment against killing reflects the utmost value we place on life, promoting a society of peace, harmony, and righteousness. By embracing this commandment, we acknowledge the sanctity of every individual's existence and contribute to a world where all are respected and protected.

Valuing life is not a mere suggestion but a fundamental principle that underpins the fabric of our society. When we uphold the sanctity of life, we foster an environment where love, compassion, and empathy thrive.

It is through our actions of non-violence and respect that we create a community built on righteousness.

By adhering to the commandment "Thou shalt not kill," we establish a foundation of trust and harmony. We recognize the inherent worth of each person, nurturing an atmosphere of empathy and understanding. In valuing life, we also create space for growth, forgiveness, and healing, embracing the potential for a brighter future for all.

How Do the Blessings Found in the 10 Commandments Reflect Philippians 4:8 When Compared to Earthly Desires and Works of the Flesh vs Spirit?

The 10 commandments serve as divine guidance vs earthly desires, promoting honesty, respect, and fidelity. Similarly, Philippians 4:8 encourages focusing on the virtuous, praiseworthy, and honorable. In contrast, earthly desires and works of the flesh can lead us astray from these divine blessings.

I want to emphasize that these Commandments are not listed in a specific order. In Roman Catholic tradition, their ranking would be as follows: 8, 4, 7, 6, 9/10, 2, 1, 3, and 5. "Thou Shall Not Covet" encompasses the 9th and 10th Commandments.

The blessings within the Ten Commandments embody principles that cultivate gratitude.

I want to conclude this chapter by sharing the joy I have found in my blessings.

The Delight Found in My Blessings

Life is an intricate weave of trials and triumphs, challenges and joys, but in the heart of it all lies an undeniable truth: blessings are abundant, and their delight is immeasurable. In moments of quiet reflection, I have come to see that the richness of my life is not measured in accolades or material gain but in the relationships, experiences, and values that have shaped me.

Among my greatest blessings is the family surrounding me with love and unwavering support. My wife's family, the Unchuans, welcomed me into their fold with open arms and hearts, teaching me the true essence of acceptance, fairness, and nurturing love. Through them, I have experienced a profound sense of belonging and unity that transcends the mere connection of marriage. Their laughter, wisdom, and faith have been a constant source of inspiration, filling my life with warmth and purpose. I have been privileged to witness the bonds that hold them together, strengthened by traditions, shared experiences, and a mutual commitment to each other's happiness. Their example has reinforced the importance of selflessness, generosity, and the joy of giving without expectation.

Fordham University, another pivotal blessing, was more than just an institution of learning --- it was the gateway to self-discovery and personal growth. The lessons I absorbed there extended beyond the classroom, instilling diligence, perseverance, and the drive to apply myself fully. When I found myself at a crossroads, uncertain about my career path, Fordham redirected my course from marketing to accounting. This decision would ultimately define my professional success. Even more significantly, it was at Fordham that I encountered a mentor, a distinguished alumnus who saw potential in me and provided me with an opportunity that laid the foundation for my career. The joy of that unexpected turn of fortune still lingers, reminding me that sometimes, the greatest blessings come disguised as gentle nudges toward a better path.

Yet, blessings are not solely confined to times of ease; they are also found in adversity. My journey through prostate cancer has been fraught with fear, uncertainty, and pain. Still, within this experience, I have unearthed profound insights. The love and concern of my family, the dedication of my doctors, and the resilience I have discovered within myself are all blessings in their own right. The ability to wake up each day, continue fighting, and hold onto hope are gifts I do not take for granted. Even in the face of illness, I have learned to find delight in the simple moments: a heartfelt conversation, a quiet sunrise, or the reassuring hand of a loved one.

One of the most unexpected joys has been the deepened connections formed during this time. Illness has a way of stripping away the distractions of life, bringing into focus what truly matters. The outpouring of love and encouragement I have received has been humbling, reminding me of the immense goodness in the people around me. Friends, family, and acquaintances have rallied around me, offering support in ways I never anticipated. It has reinforced my belief in the power of human kindness and the importance of being present for others in their times of need.

Perhaps the most significant lesson I have learned is that gratitude magnifies the delight in one's blessings. When I focus on what I have rather than what I lack, my heart is filled with a sense of peace that no hardship can shake. The joy in blessings is about acknowledging them and fully embracing and cherishing them. It is recognizing that I am surrounded by love, faith, and purpose, even through trials.

Life's blessings, big and small, weave together to create a rich and meaningful existence. In them, I find delight, and in delight, I see the strength to move forward with gratitude and hope. The journey of life is not without its hardships. Still, the awareness of our blessings transforms struggles into stepping stones, allowing us to appreciate the depth of our experiences and the beauty of the love surrounding us.

9

Express thanks

"As we express our gratitude, we must never forget that the highest appreciation is not to utter words but to live by them."
—John F. Kennedy.

"At times, our own light goes out and is rekindled by a spark from another person. Each of us has cause to think with deep gratitude of those who have lighted the flame within us."
—Albert Schweitzer.

"Silent gratitude isn't very much use to anyone."
—Gertrude Stein.

"Thanksgiving Day is a good day to recommit our energies to giving thanks and just giving."
—Amy Grant.

In a world that often emphasizes ambition, achievement, and the pursuit of more, gratitude is a quiet yet transformative force. Giving thanks is not merely a polite social convention but a profound practice that can shape our perspective, relationships, and overall well-being. From ancient spiritual traditions to modern scientific research, gratitude has been recognized as a key to happiness, resilience, and success. This chapter explores the power of giving thanks and how it can positively impact our lives.

The Science Behind Gratitude

Studies in psychology and neuroscience have revealed that expressing gratitude activates areas of the brain associated with happiness and emotional regulation. When we give thanks, our brain releases dopamine and serotonin, neurotransmitters that promote feelings of pleasure and contentment. Regularly practicing gratitude can even rewire our brains, making us more inclined to notice and appreciate the positive aspects of life. Research also shows that grateful individuals experience lower levels of stress and depression, improved sleep quality, and more substantial immune function.

Neuroscientific studies using brain imaging have demonstrated that gratitude activates the prefrontal cortex, the brain region associated with decision-making, emotional regulation, and social cognition. This finding suggests that gratitude improves mood and enhances our ability to make thoughtful, positive choices. Additionally, gratitude has been linked to lower cortisol levels, the hormone associated with stress, and increased heart rate variability, indicating a healthier autonomic nervous system and a more remarkable ability to handle stress effectively.

Psychologists have also found that practicing gratitude can lead to long-term changes in brain structure. A study published in *NeuroImage* found that individuals who engaged in daily gratitude exercises showed increased gray matter density in brain regions related to emotional processing and empathy. Another study conducted at the University of California, Berkeley, found that participants who wrote gratitude letters experienced heightened activity in the medial prefrontal cortex, even weeks after their gratitude practice ended, suggesting lasting positive effects on brain function.

Furthermore, gratitude influences our social interactions by strengthening neural pathways associated with trust and empathy. Expressing appreciation towards others increases oxytocin levels, sometimes called the "love hormone," which fosters feelings of connection and reduces social anxiety. This biological response explains why gratitude is crucial in building and maintaining strong, supportive relationships.

Strengthening Relationships Through Gratitude

Gratitude plays a crucial role in fostering and maintaining strong relationships. When we express appreciation to others, it reinforces bonds and encourages mutual kindness. In personal relationships, acknowledging the efforts and presence of loved ones cultivates a deeper connection and reduces misunderstandings. In professional settings, a culture of gratitude enhances teamwork, motivation, and overall workplace satisfaction.

In romantic relationships, regularly expressing gratitude strengthens emotional intimacy and trust. Studies have shown that couples who practice gratitude experience higher relationship satisfaction and can better navigate conflicts. Simple acts such as saying "thank you" for everyday gestures, recognizing each other's contributions, and expressing appreciation for support can significantly improve relational harmony.

Friendships also benefit from gratitude, as it fosters loyalty and mutual respect. When we make an effort to show appreciation for our friends' presence, kindness, and efforts, it strengthens the bond and creates a positive cycle of goodwill. Acknowledging small acts of kindness, such as a friend checking in or offering help, builds more vigorous, more enduring connections.

In professional environments, gratitude fosters a positive workplace culture, increasing morale and reducing burnout. Employees who feel appreciated by their colleagues and supervisors are more engaged, motivated, and productive. Recognizing the hard work of coworkers, providing constructive praise, and creating an environment where gratitude is a shared value lead to greater collaboration and job satisfaction.

Communities and social groups also thrive when gratitude is a common practice. When individuals feel valued and recognized for their contributions, they are more likely to engage and contribute positively. Acts of gratitude, such as acknowledging volunteers, expressing appreciation for neighbors, or recognizing community leaders' efforts, strengthen society's fabric and encourage a culture of kindness and cooperation.

Gratitude In Times Of Adversity

While it is easy to be thankful when life is smooth, gratitude's true power shines in difficult times. Challenges and setbacks are an inevitable part of life. Still, gratitude helps us shift our focus from what is lacking to what remains. It fosters resilience by allowing us to find meaning in hardships, appreciate lessons learned, and recognize the support around us. Even in moments of pain and uncertainty, there is always something to be thankful for—a lesson, a kind word, or the simple gift of another day.

Gratitude in adversity does not mean ignoring pain or hardship; instead, it offers a way to reframe challenges. It helps us recognize inner strength, the kindness of others, and the growth that comes through perseverance. Research has shown that individuals who practice gratitude during difficult times experience lower levels of anxiety and depression, as well as a greater sense of hope and emotional resilience.

During periods of loss, gratitude can serve as a source of healing. Remembering the positive memories, the love shared, and the support received can provide comfort and perspective. Many people who have faced hardships, including illness, financial struggles, or personal losses, find solace in focusing on what remains rather than what is lost.

One powerful way to cultivate gratitude in adversity is to seek out silver linings. Even in the most challenging circumstances, there are often unexpected moments of kindness, new opportunities for growth, or the chance to develop a deeper appreciation for life's simple blessings. Expressing gratitude for small victories, a supportive community, or lessons learned can provide a sense of purpose and strength.

Ways To Cultivate Gratitude (A Review)

1. Keeping a Gratitude Journal – Writing down things we are grateful for each day helps reinforce a habit of appreciation. It allows us to reflect on the good in our lives.
2. Expressing Appreciation – Taking time to thank others, whether through a verbal acknowledgment, a written note, or a simple gesture, strengthens relationships and spreads positivity.
3. Practicing Mindfulness – Being present and savoring the moment helps us recognize the beauty and blessings in our daily experiences.
4. Shifting Perspective – When faced with challenges, reframing situations to focus on what can be learned or gained fosters a grateful outlook.
5. Serving Others – Acts of kindness and generosity benefit others and deepen our gratitude by reminding us of what we have to give.

A Personal Story: How Expressing Thanks Enhanced My Life

There was a time when I took many things for granted --- the support of loved ones, the opportunities I had, and the simple joys of daily life. It wasn't until I faced one of the most significant challenges of my life --- my battle with prostate cancer --- that I truly understood the power of gratitude.

When I received my diagnosis, my initial reaction was fear and uncertainty. However, as I navigated the journey of treatment and recovery, I made a conscious effort to express gratitude. I thanked my doctors and nurses for their care and expertise. I expressed appreciation to my family for their unwavering support. I even found gratitude in small moments, like a friend's encouraging words or a beautiful sunrise on a difficult morning.

As I embraced this practice, I noticed a shift in my perspective. Instead of focusing on what I had lost, I began to see what I had gained --- more profound relationships, newfound resilience, and an appreciation for life's fragility. Gratitude became a source of strength, helping me endure the most demanding days and celebrate the victories, no matter how small.

Today, I continue to live with gratitude, knowing that every day is a gift. Thanks have improved my outlook, deepened my connections with others, and renewed my sense of purpose. Gratitude, I have learned, is not just about acknowledging the good in life --- it is about finding light even in the darkest moments.

Conclusion

Giving thanks is more than an occasional act; it is a way of life. It can transform our mindset, strengthen our relationships, and enhance our well-being. Whether in moments of joy or adversity, gratitude provides a steady foundation, reminding us that even in an imperfect world, there is always something to be thankful for.

By embracing gratitude, we cultivate a sense of abundance rather than scarcity, recognizing the richness of our lives beyond material possessions. It fosters humility, reminding us that much of what we have is made possible by the kindness, support, and efforts of others. We become more present, compassionate, and resilient through gratitude in life's inevitable ups and downs.

Ultimately, gratitude is a gift that multiplies the more it is shared. It has the potential to create a ripple effect, spreading positivity and warmth to those around us. By making gratitude a daily practice, we elevate our lives and contribute to a more kind, connected, and hopeful world—one thank-you at a time.

10

THE ENDING IS JUST A NEW BEGINNING

As I reflect on the journey that has brought me to this moment, I see a life shaped by the people I've met, the choices I've made, and the challenges I've faced. Gratitude has been my guiding force --- allowing me to appreciate the lessons of the past while embracing the uncertainties of the future.

Looking back, I understand that every hardship, every triumph, and every moment of doubt has played a role in shaping the person I am today. The love of family, the wisdom of experience, and the values instilled by those who walked beside me have given my life meaning and purpose.

But as this book ends, I recognize that endings are never indeed the end. They are merely transitions --- turning points that lead us into the next chapter of our story. Life continues to unfold, offering new opportunities for growth, love, and gratitude.

So, while I have spent these pages looking in the rearview mirror, I now turn my gaze forward. The road ahead is unwritten, and I welcome it with the same faith and appreciation that have carried me this far. Because in the grand journey of life, every ending is just a new beginning.

I am grateful to everyone who has been a part of my life and to those who take the time to read this book.

FINAL THOUGHTS

I wrote this book to highlight the transformative power of gratitude and self-reflection. By sharing my personal experiences, I aim to demonstrate how these practices have positively shaped my life. Embracing these principles requires continuous effort and dedication. While I still have much to learn and grow, gratitude has already enriched my life and the lives of those around me.

Gratitude is more than just an attitude toward people and circumstances. It is a model for others, inspiring them to follow your example. It fosters values that deepen one's connection to a higher power and reinforces a lesson I learned from Mama Kitty: that my journey and those I encounter will be safe and meaningful if guided by LOVE and THE GOLDEN RULE.

Some core values cultivated through gratitude include honesty, respect, collaboration, appreciation, empathy, compassion, kindness, understanding, optimism, resilience, and confidence. Committing to these relationship-strengthening principles equips you with the tools to make a lasting impact on yourself, your family, and your community.

I can only hope that our leaders—at the city, state, and federal levels, including the Office of the President, the U.S. Congress, and the federal courts, especially the Supreme Court—reflect on these principles and uphold them in their service. They must remember that they represent all of us, not just themselves or their political affiliations.

www.ingramcontent.com/pod-product-compliance
Lightning Source LLC
Chambersburg PA
CBHW051217120626
46547CB00013B/1392